▼

CLEAN & SOBER PARENTING

A Guide to Help Recovering Parents

How to Order:

Quantity discounts are available from Prima Publishing, Post Office Box 1260NEL, Rocklin, CA 95677; telephone (916) 786-0449. On your letterhead include information concerning the intended use of the books and the number of books you wish to purchase.

▼
_____

CLEAN & SOBER PARENTING
A Guide to Help Recovering Parents

Dear Mother & Dad —
Love Riki

Jane Nelsen, Riki Intner, and Lynn Lott

Prima Publishing
P. O. Box 1260NEL
Rocklin, CA 95677
(916) 786-0426

Production by Carol Dondrea, Bookman Productions
Typography by Hi-Tech Graphics & Publishing
Copyediting by Linda Purrington
Interior design by Renee Deprey
Jacket design by The Dunlavey Studio
Cover photo by Dan Mills

Prima Publishing
Rocklin, CA

Library of Congress Cataloging-in-Publication Data
Nelsen, Jane.
  Clean & sober parenting: a guide to help recovering parents /
Jane Nelsen, Riki Intner, Lynn Lott.
    p. cm.
  Includes index.
  ISBN 1-55958-165-4
  1. Children of alcoholics. 2. Parenting. 3. Alcoholics—
Rehabilitation. I. Intner, Riki. II. Lott, Lynn. III. Title.
IV. Title: Clean and sober parenting.
HV5133.N43 1992
362.29′13—dc20   92-20874
                                                          CIP

92 93 94 95 RRD 10 9 8 7 6 5 4 3 2 1

Printed in the United States of America

To Alfred Adler and Rudolf Dreikurs with deep gratitude for their substantial influence in our lives and in our work. And thanks to the people who were willing to bare their souls and share their stories so others could learn from their experiences.

▼
_____

Contents

▼

Foreword

H. Stephen Glenn

The decade of the 1980s saw the emergence of co-dependency treatment as the major movement in the recovery field. The co-dependency treatment movement began with adult children of alcoholics and progressed through family dysfunction of all kinds. During most of the decade, the focus was on individual recovery and healing. It generated tremendous insights about the conflict between the inner child and the outer adult. So far, many people have failed to go beyond recovery to discover new patterns of parenting and family relationships that promote health and well-being. This will be the major work of the 1990s and beyond.

Clean and Sober Parenting takes us beyond recovery into the essential areas of repatterning and recreating family dynamics and parenting styles that produce natural growth. All too frequently, people go through recovery to get help with an acute drug problem. They go through treatment and assume that, with recovery, their current relationships and family will significantly improve. This often doesn't occur, because the only "tapes" and programs people have to work from frequently reflect generational patterns of dysfunction and inadequacy, which may leave the family or the primary relationships unaltered.

Such people often bond to their recovery group as a surrogate family, at the expense of their primary relationships and family. *Clean and Sober Parenting* provides a model for relationships that eliminates these dichotomies and helps people work along a healthy continuum. It provides hope, encouragement, and alternatives that empower people and their relationships.

The authors have drawn on extensive backgrounds in family counseling, therapy, parent training, and drug treatment. They provide an unusually well-focused and challenging discussion of crucial issues, conflicts, and solutions that are central to the health and well-being of every human being. This makes the book important for *everyone*, whether from a dysfunctional background or not.

The rate and intensity of change in today's society and the loss of sociocultural support systems have rendered many of our traditional assumptions about and approaches to raising children and maintaining families and relationships obsolete. In nearly every human endeavor, we acknowledge the need for constant updating and adaptation, but we've been very slow to acknowledge this same need for families and relationships. *Clean and Sober Parenting* offers a process and set of guidelines for responding to this challenge on an ongoing basis, which makes it a must for everyone who cares about people and the discovery process for empowering personal and family growth.

H. Stephen Glenn, President
Developing Capable People Associates

▼
_____

Introduction

This book is for people in recovery who have children and who want to break the unhealthy, discouraging patterns of relating that are created by chemical abuse. This book is also for adult children of alcoholics, for people in the helping professions who are working with recovering families, and for people who are not abusing drugs but who, while parenting their children, are living with someone who is abusing alcohol and drugs. This book can help you take charge of your life, develop a new picture of what expectations are realistic, and make changes that bring health and healing to the whole family. One step at a time, you can learn to create order and consistency with your children, instead of the chaos that was created while you were using chemicals.

This book looks at recovery as a process. Too often, family members expect that when the drinking and drug abuse stops, all problems will disappear and they will live happily ever after. They are often dismayed and deeply disappointed to find that it doesn't work that way. But parents often come into early recovery with few if any parenting skills. In fact, some parents started abusing chemicals when they were just kids themselves. They missed out on many of the lessons that a nonabusing person might learn through normal growth and development.

Parents in recovery desperately need effective parenting skills. During the time of their chemical dependency, they abused and/or neglected their children. When they become clean and sober, they are left with feelings of guilt and shame over what they have done to their children. This often leads to overcompensation in the form of letting children manipulate them to get special service and undue attention to "make up" for the terrible things that have been done to them.

Such a relationship is not healthy for parents or children. Parents who give their children special service and undue attention usually feel overwhelmed and resentful, which leads to more guilt and shame. It is a vicious cycle. The children learn unproductive manipulation skills rather than productive skills of taking responsibility, cooperating, contributing, and developing self-esteem. Ineffective parenting increases guilt and shame and burdens parents with the demands of dependent, insecure, acting-out children. Effective parenting skills are essential to break these unproductive cycles.

Recovering parents want to be *good* parents, but they have been focused on chemical abuse, not on guiding and nurturing their children. Now they need to learn parenting skills such as listening and talking in respectful ways. Recovering family members have been out of touch with their feelings and need to learn how to express feelings and listen to the feelings of others. This approach challenges the unspoken rules that governed the family before recovery: "Don't talk, don't feel, and don't trust"— identified by Claudia Black in her book, *It Will Never Happen to Me* (1981). Recovering parents also need to learn how to create structure and routine where previously only chaos existed.

Chemical dependency and co-dependency create feelings of deep discouragement in families. In an atmosphere of chaos, inconsistency, distrust, and denial, unhealthy patterns spring up and become established. By improving their parenting skills, parents can encourage healing for their family while they are beginning to heal themselves.

In this book, we give many examples of the help people have received from parenting classes and workshops. We strongly suggest you find a parenting education support group that offers you a safe place to practice the many skills we teach in this book.

Some parents fear that trying to improve parenting skills will be too overwhelming while they are giving up their drug dependence. In early recovery, they are often told not to concentrate on anything except their recovery. We do not believe that deferring the process of learning new parenting skills is a real option. After all, the kids don't disappear just because their parents are in recovery. And ignoring the kids or continuing ineffective parenting practices actually makes recovery more difficult.

While you are reading *Clean and Sober Parenting*, it is important to stay in the role of a learner and use the information to help you grow. Anyone can make a mistake; the measure of recovery is whether you use those mistakes to learn and grow, or to beat yourself up and to blame others. When you follow the guidelines described in this book, you can feel good about being with your kids and being in a family.

We, the authors, have worked extensively with parents in the recovery process. We have found that learning and practicing parenting skills while in recovery enhances the recovery process. Parents feel much better about themselves when they are being effective with their children. And when children are more responsible, cooperative, and contributing members of the family, parents have more time and energy for recovery.

Following the suggestions in *Clean and Sober Parenting* can give you hope, help you eliminate guilt and shame from the past, and help you look forward to the future, one day at a time, with confidence and skills. This book gives you the opportunity to work on your individual issues, recognize the mistakes you have made, and learn that mistakes are part of life and the learning process. You can learn how to make amends to your children, stop judging yourself and others, and feel more connected with your children. You'll find out you are not alone, nor are you a terrible parent. You'll learn that you have value and can begin to take responsibility for yourself while helping those around you take responsibility for their own behavior.

▼
_____

CLEAN & SOBER PARENTING

A Guide to Help Recovering Parents

Chapter

1

Start Where You Are and Keep It Simple

As you begin reading this book, perhaps you have just quit abusing drugs or alcohol. Maybe you have been to a few AA, NA, or Al-Anon meetings. Perhaps you've been in recovery for some time, but still feel overwhelmed by all the messes created by chemical abuse in your family. Or you may be one of the many people recovering from co-dependency.

No matter where you start, it is possible to overcome the effects of chemical dependency in the family, pick up the pieces, and make things better than before. Yes, we said, "better than before." Your crisis with chemical dependency could be a blessing in disguise, an opportunity to become aware of the need for improvement — especially in parenting skills.

Chemical dependency does not cause ineffective parenting. A lack of effective parenting skills is not uncommon in families without chemical dependency. However, many people are not even aware that their

1

parenting skills are ineffective because they don't experience a crisis that could motivate them to grow and improve.

Look for the Possible Good in Every Situation

Children growing up with parents who are substance abusers or co-dependents experience extremely unfavorable circumstances. This can be a plus or a minus. We don't mean to diminish the pain experienced by these children. However, many people have used unfavorable circumstances to learn and grow. Some develop a sense of compassion, spirituality, and a desire to help others. Some develop a strong determination to avoid the mistakes of their parents and to learn what characteristics can lead them to success in business and/or in their personal lives. Others, unfortunately, use unfavorable circumstances as an excuse to *stop* learning and growing. *It is not what happens to us, but what we decide about it, that determines the course of our lives.* When circumstances are tough, a wide variety of decisions are possible. Some people decide, "Life is unfair; I should feel sorry for myself; I will never amount to anything" or "I will get even." Others decide, "Life is a challenge; I can handle it." Some decide to be victims of their fate; others decide to be masters.

Adult Attitudes Influence Children's Attitudes

If you adopt attitudes of guilt and shame, it is likely that your children will follow your lead. If you adopt attitudes of hope and optimism, however, again your children will probably follow. Your attitudes about yourselves and the future can have a tremendously clear impact on the decisions your children make.

Children of substance abusers and co-dependents often make decisions—about themselves, about life, and about others—that do not lead to helpful, happy, productive lives. But *Clean and Sober Parenting* offers everyone an opportunity to make new decisions. In this book, we are sending you a message of hope and possibility.

Rejecting a Victim Mentality

It is *never* too late to change decisions and attitudes and take a new direction. Too many people get bogged down in guilt and shame and adopt a victim mentality. We keep saying this over and over because it's something all recovering parents need to hear again and again, and we'll go on saying it. First, let's explain what we mean by "victim mentality."

People who develop a victim mentality spend most of their time thinking of themselves as victims, focusing on past injustices and blaming others or circumstances. They use these injustices and circumstances to invent excuses for not taking charge of their lives. They spend their lives reacting to the past instead of acting in the present. People who develop a victim mentality focus on the *reasons* for their problems instead of on *solutions*. You do not want to create a victim mentality in yourselves or your children by hanging on to guilt and shame. Yes, you did create pain and mistrust during the dependency and co-dependency period. But recovery is the time to learn from mistakes, adopt attitudes and skills to create change, and build trust in yourselves and your children.

Although many scars are left by crises of drug abuse, the only way to make things better is to start change somewhere and take one step at a time. With this approach, even the most overwhelming "messes" can eventually disappear.

Our optimistic attitude does not mean we minimize the devastating effects of chemical abuse on children. Children in chemically dependent families have lived with neglect, abuse, inconsistency, disappointment, and loneliness. They are waiting for their parents to make it better. In some families, the children have been parenting the family, and it may be a shock to them when their parents suddenly take an active parenting role again. At first it may be difficult for them to give up the leadership to their parents, but they really would prefer to be children and have a childhood. In *Clean and Sober Parenting*, we teach ways to include instead of exclude children as parents reassume leadership. Still, it is helpful to understand children's resistance to such change. It is ironic how often human beings resist change even when they are miserable. When you understand this, you can expect resistance and still move toward long-range goals.

Moving toward the long-range goal of effective parenting in recovery does not mean that you can or must achieve perfection. The growing process includes steps forward and backward. It takes courage to keep the long-range goal in mind even when we have setbacks. We have never known anyone (ourselves included) who did not make progress, regress, grow, make mistakes, learn from the mistakes and improve, backslide, and then move forward again. It is all part of the growing process.

Don't get too discouraged when you experience the downs (although some discouragement is natural). Knowing that ups and downs are normal can help. Taking one step at a time means working on improvement, not perfection, and seeing mistakes as opportunities to learn.

Some people think a responsible person is one who never makes mistakes. Our definition of a responsible person is someone who takes responsibility for his or her mistakes, learns from mistakes, and repairs the damage when possible.

Mistakes as Opportunities to Learn

At the foundation of guilt and shame are the crazy notions about mistakes that have been perpetuated in our society. At our workshops we often ask, "What were you taught about mistakes?" These are a few of the typical answers we get:

"Mistakes are bad."

"You shouldn't make mistakes."

"You are stupid, bad, inadequate, or a failure if you make mistakes."

"If you make a mistake, don't let anyone find out. If they do find out, make up an excuse even if it isn't true."

We call these notions about mistakes *crazy,* because they damage self-esteem and breed depression and discouragement. It is difficult to learn and grow when we feel discouraged. We all know of people who have made mistakes and then dug themselves into a deeper hole by trying to cover up the mistake. We also know how forgiving people can be when others admit their mistakes, apologize, and try to solve the problems created by the mistake.

We need to change these crazy notions about mistakes, and instead teach our children that mistakes are wonderful opportunities to learn. Every person in the world will continue to make mistakes all his or her life. Since this is true, it is healthier to see mistakes as opportunities to learn instead of as proof of inadequacy. When people react to mistakes with blame, guilt, and shame, they are in danger of pushing their children into developing a victim mentality. Once you understand the dangers of developing a victim mentality and the importance of seeing mistakes as opportunities to learn, looking at your past will be a different experience. It can be a simple step that can give you information to help you move forward.

In the following case, we show how Myra began to recover and started taking steps to heal herself and her family. Myra found her crisis with chemical dependency to be a blessing in disguise. When she saw the need for improving her parenting, she made many of the attitude changes we have been describing. As you read about Myra, notice how she gave up her victim mentality and faced her resistance to change. By accepting that recovery is a process with ups and downs, Myra could start healing the scars of chemical abuse one step at a time.

Getting Help

Myra and Cliff had two young girls, 9-year-old Becky and 6-year-old Cheryl. They had a small suburban house, and both parents worked, Myra as a nurse, Cliff as a hearing aid salesman. Myra had a sister in the area; Cliff's relatives all lived in the East.

One day Myra and her neighbor were having coffee. The neighbor noticed Myra was sweating and shaking. She could see how miserable Myra was, but she didn't know what to do. She called a friend who was a nurse at a local drug treatment center and asked her to talk to Myra. The nurse recognized the signs of narcotic withdrawal and recommended that Myra get into a treatment program immediately.

Myra decided she was in over her head and knew she would go to jail if she didn't stop using. She had been writing her own prescriptions and was addicted to Vicodin. She was relieved that her friend helped her take the first step to get outpatient treatment.

According to Myra, her life was terrible before she started treatment. She was on edge all the time, in constant fear, and lying to everyone. Besides the Vicodin, she was also using cocaine. Myra described the drugging as the worst time of her life. She used while she was pregnant and while nursing. She would stay up and party all night and couldn't get to work or get the kids to school the next day. She was forever making excuses to have her friends take the kids, saying she was sick. She was always irritable, edgy, and inconsistent with Becky and Cheryl. If they dropped or spilled something, one time she would say, "It's OK," and the next time next she would yell and scream.

In the first week of recovery, Myra felt racked with guilt. She had made so many poor choices for herself that she felt she had no right to make choices for her daughters. As a result, her husband now had to take on all the responsibility for parenting. Myra was so scared that she asked Cliff to take a week off work to take care of the children. During that first week, she could barely function as an individual, much less as a parent.

It was important for Myra to start where she was; she needed help and couldn't do everything herself. But the rest of the family also needed help. A counselor in the treatment center suggested that Myra had enough to do just to begin her healing process, and recommended that the other family members join support groups offered by the center. Cliff decided to attend a Narc-Anon group to deal with his co-dependency issues. And Cliff enrolled Becky and Cheryl in a kids' group, where they started to learn more about what had been happening in their family.

Honesty and Information

Parents need to be honest with their kids about what has been happening. A simple first step is to make sure the kids get information about chemical dependency from an educated source. Myra and Cliff enrolled their daughters in a kids' group, where they learned to define and use words such as *alcoholic, drug addict, co-dependent,* and *blackout.* Giving kids information about what has been going on is a relief to them. They can now see the family had a problem, and that *they* were not the problem and were not responsible for fixing it.

It is helpful when the nonusing parent is willing to be honest about how he or she might have been contributing to the problem through co-dependent and enabling behaviors, and how he or she can be part of the solution and recovery. (A *dependent* person focuses on a drug. A *co-dependent* focuses on a drug-dependent person. The *enabling behaviors* of a co-dependent include rescuing, fixing, excusing, nagging, spying, threatening, blaming, and denying the seriousness of the problem.) Cliff was willing to consider his co-dependency issues and got help from his Narc-Anon group to work on his own recovery.

With her counselor in the outpatient treatment program, Myra began the painful process of reviewing the past. She realized her drugging was abusive to Becky and Cheryl and created an environment that invited feelings of insecurity. Myra saw that Becky acted out her insecurity by making bedtime miserable. Instead of going to sleep or staying in her room, she'd get up continually to check and see if her parents were OK. Cheryl acted out her insecurity by reacting in an overly sensitive way to noises and acting meek and clingy. She'd panic even if one of her parents walked out of the house to go to the garage. Although they couldn't express what they felt in words, Becky and Cheryl picked up the stress in the family and lived in constant fear that something bad might happen to their parents.

Becky and Cheryl had experienced severe neglect. Cliff neglected them because he was busy worrying about Myra. And Myra was too drugged to follow through on parenting routines with her daughters. She was not "present" enough to give them quality time or anything else children need from a parent. Becky and Cheryl both chose behaviors that they perceived would help them survive: one girl kept both parents busy with her at bedtime, and the other reacted overly sensitively, to get their attention.

Myra felt guilty about her chemical abuse and about neglecting her children. She blamed herself for their behavior. And one of the most painful things Myra had to face was that the beginning of recovery did not mean the end of problems.

Recovery Is a Beginning

Too often people believe that ending abuse will end the problems. But normal problems and poor life skills are overshadowed by the problems of abuse. For example, Myra and Cliff lacked parenting skills even before she began to abuse chemicals. It would not make sense to think they would become excellent parents the moment Myra stopped abusing and Cliff stopped his co-dependent behaviors.

When Myra stopped drugging, many of her life skill problems surfaced. She had many control issues and overly high expectations not only for herself but also for the people she lived with. According to Myra, she was demanding, rigid, and a perfectionist. Myra didn't want to parent if she couldn't be the *perfect* parent. She was angry with her kids if they didn't do all their homework, get good grades, and get along with each other at all times. Fortunately, once in recovery Myra realized that, like all people, she wasn't born with parenting skills and that she needed to be educated. So she and Cliff joined a parenting class.

Parent Education Speeds the Recovery Process

People in our society have accepted the need for education for just about every role except parenting. Too many people think parenting should come "naturally." We, on the contrary, believe parent education is extremely important. It has made a tremendous difference in our personal lives and in the lives of thousands of other parents lucky enough to discover parent education classes. We believe it is especially important for people in recovery who want to repair the damage their chemical dependency has done to their children and to make things better than before.

Before recovery and parent education, Myra and Cliff were very negative and ineffective with their daughters. For instance, when Becky didn't want to stay in her room at bedtime, Myra and Cliff would begin by escorting her back to her room. When Becky kept coming out of her room, they would lose their patience and start yelling at her to stay in bed. In their parenting class, they learned several "keep it simple" skills that improved life with their daughters and helped Becky and Cheryl make changes about how they could belong in the family through cooperative behavior instead of misbehavior.

Use Fewer Words

Myra and Cliff learned to stop using so many words and learned to practice being brief and clear. The next time Becky came out of her room after bedtime, they said, "It's bedtime and you need to go to bed." The first night Becky got out of bed three times. Instead of getting angry, they repeated the same phrase, kindly and firmly, each time. When they refused to argue, get mad, or get involved beyond their simple phrase, Becky eventually went to her room and stayed there. Now Myra and Cliff both felt less stressed and more hopeful.

Maintain Dignity and Respect

Myra and Cliff also learned to change how they handled conflicts with Becky and Cheryl. In the drugging days, Myra lacked tolerance for conflict of any kind. When Becky and Cheryl got into fights, Myra would scream at them. Now she and Cliff deal with conflict by treating themselves and the girls respectfully. They decide what they are willing to do (respect for themselves) and enforce agreements with kindness and firmness (respect for the girls). When the girls fight, Myra will say, "I do not like to listen to fighting. If you want to fight, go outside." If the girls object, she kindly and firmly repeats, "Outside."

11

Respect Individuality

Myra and Cliff learned the importance of noticing and respecting the individuality of the girls. At family meetings, they planned individual time on their calendars for each girl with each parent. They discussed bedtimes and agreed with Becky that since she was older she could stay up a little later than Cheryl. When Cheryl complained that it was unfair for her to go to bed earlier than her sister, Cliff replied, "'When she was your age, she went to bed earlier. When you are older, you will have a later bedtime." As Becky and Cheryl felt more valued as individuals, the frequency and intensity of their conflicts diminished.

Give Choices

Myra noticed the kids were more cooperative if given choices. Before learning this, she had not realized how she invited resistance when she gave orders. Now Myra found it simple to ask, "Do you want to turn the television off at 7:30 or 8:00?" The first time Myra offered this choice, Cheryl said, "I don't want to turn off the television." Myra was kind and firm when she replied, "That is not one of the choices. You can choose 7:30 or 8:00, or I will turn the television off now."

Other choices included, "You decide how much time you need to get ready in the morning. Then you can choose between the alarm clock and me to wake you up." "Do you want to be ready when I leave and ride with me, or get ready later and walk?" "Do you want to do your homework right after school, or right after dinner?" When the girls got older, she gave broader choices: "Do you want to do your homework, or do you want to experience the consequences of not doing your homework?"

When the choices weren't effective, Myra no longer saw this outcome as a failure. Instead, she would go back to using fewer words to enforce rules and agreements with dignity and respect, or get the girls involved in communication and problem solving. Her parenting class had helped her change her beliefs about perfection and mistakes.

Change Attitudes About Mistakes

Myra loved learning about mistakes as wonderful opportunities to learn and grow. It helpled her focus on progress instead of perfection. This helped in her recovery by removing the pressure of having to fix everything immediately, and it gave her hope for the future.

She said that before she started recovery she always thought she had to protect her children from making mistakes and from the hurt of those mistakes. Myra grew up believing it is not OK to make a mistake. Of course, she made many mistakes, so she learned to hide them when she could. Her parenting class helped her see this had not been healthy for her. She had not realized before that her parents' attitude about mistakes taught her to be sneaky and try to hide her mistakes. She did not want to repeat this pattern with her children.

Hiding mistakes keeps people isolated and suffering from a lack of feedback from others. You can't fix mistakes that are hidden, nor learn from them. Trying to prevent mistakes keeps people rigid and fearful. But we're all human, so we'll all make mistakes, and mistakes give everyone opportunities to try again and learn from experience. As the saying goes, "Good judgment comes from experience, and experience comes from poor judgment." (We found this quote scribbled on a restroom wall at the Squeeze Inn Restaurant in Truckee, California.) Myra learned that trying to prevent children from making mistakes doesn't help them learn and grow.

Sometimes mistakes require that people make amends where possible, and at least apologize when amends are not possible. Myra learned about the "Three R's of Recovery" in her parenting class and decided to use this method to apologize to her daughters for some of the mistakes she couldn't change.

The Three R's of Recovery from Mistakes

1. Recognize the mistake with a feeling of responsibility instead of blame.
2. Reconcile by apologizing to the people you have offended during your mistake.
3. Resolve the problem, when possible, by working together on a solution together.

Myra told Becky and Cheryl, "When I was abusing drugs, I yelled at you one minute and ignored you the next. That was a mistake. I was edgy from the drugs and paying more attention to them than I was to you. I am really sorry."

The girls said, "That's OK, Mom." (It is typical for children to be forgiving when we take responsibility for our mistakes, even though they may be very angry when we are not taking responsibility.)

Myra said, "It is not OK, but I appreciate your willingness to forgive me. That will help me forgive myself. Now we need to work on ways to solve the problems that were created while I was using drugs. Are you willing to help me solve the problems that have been created in our family?"

Both girls said, "Yes."

Myra said, "It will take time to solve the problems. There are so many. I would like to suggest that we have regular family meetings once a week. How does that sound to you?"

Family Meetings

One of the girls asked, "What is a family meeting?"

Myra answered, "We will put a blank piece of paper on the refrigerator. It will be called the *agenda*. All of us can put anything on the agenda that we would like to discuss or to solve. Then during the family meeting we will talk about things on the agenda. First we will start every meeting with compliments and appreciations. That means we will look for good things to say about each other at the beginning of each meeting."

Becky and Cheryl were excited; they exclaimed, "That sounds great. Let's do it." (For more information on family meetings, see Chapter 7.)

Myra and Cliff found life became simpler when the girls were involved in solving problems and communicating in family meetings. Myra wondered, "Why did I ever think I had to do everything myself?" Learning these skills helped Myra and Cliff see that recovery can provide an excellent opportunity to heal and grow that is missed by many people who live "normal" lives.

Work for Improvement and Not Perfection

Both Cliff and Myra modeled "keeping it simple" and "growing step by step." Instead of striving for perfection, they took small steps toward improvement. A perfectionistic attitude is discouraging because it is unrealistic. Change is usually accomplished gradually, not overnight.

Expecting perfection sets people up for failure. Trying to be perfect goes against human nature. It's a losing battle, coupled with pain and stress. In fact, many people started using chemicals in the first place to cover up the painful feelings that accompanied their feelings of low self-worth if they couldn't be perfect. Recovery and improved parenting skills provide an opportunity to become better than before the chemical abuse, because they provide a realistic understanding of the change and growth process.

Drug abuse is a crisis that robs many children of a childhood. They can reclaim their childhood once their parents commit to make some changes. When you focus on progress, you are admitting that there is no "finish line," just life to be lived. Start where you are, take one step at a time, and keep it simple. With that attitude, each day provides opportunities for growth.

Chapter

2

Build Closeness and Trust Through Emotional Honesty

The skill of being emotionally honest is so helpful for healing the scars of chemical dependency and building closeness and trust that we are devoting an entire chapter to it. If we could learn only one thing to improve our parenting and build trust with our kids, we would choose to learn emotional honesty.

Emotional honesty, in the simplest form, means that it is OK to be whoever you are, think the way you think, feel the way you feel, and communicate this to others. Once you accept yourself, you can help your children know it is OK for them to be who they are, feel the way they do, and to communicate their feelings to others.

Feelings give people valuable information, just like the warning lights on a car dashboard. When you drive a car and a warning light flashes, you pay attention to it. If you want your car to last, you do what needs to be done to remedy the situation. You don't say, "That's a bad light and it shouldn't flash." This doesn't mean you feel thrilled to have the problem, but the quicker you accept the reality of what is, without judgment, the quicker you will take care of the problem.

If you feel lonely or depressed and you listen to that feeling (like paying attention to the red light on the dashboard), you get access to valuable information. Some people don't want to listen to their feelings because they believe they "shouldn't" feel the way they feel, or that they can't do anything about it, so it is easier not to know. That makes about as much sense as covering the dashboard because you believe the car "shouldn't" have problems, or because you think you can't do anything about the problems anyway. The sooner you accept a feeling without judging it, the quicker you can do something about it. You might spend a day in bed under the covers, tell a friend, or get some help. What you do isn't as important as accepting how you feel and that it's OK to feel how you feel.

When your kids are angry or resentful and they express it, the sooner you listen to their feelings without trying to make them wrong, explain away their feelings, or try to fix things for them, the easier it is to take the action that will rebuild trust in the family. We know it isn't easy. When faced with anger, most people want to defend, explain, fix, or attack. Accepting feelings can be especially difficult when there is a history of distrust in the family.

When parents go into recovery, it may take a while for kids to believe their parents will be there for them. Parents need to be brave and expect pain as they deal with the pain their children have been experiencing. Building trust takes time and consistent parent behavior.

When parents decide to change their behavior, it usually takes a while for kids to trust the changes.

Some parents get discouraged when they try to build trust through emotional honesty and their kids respond with anger. Instead of knowing this is a normal response at the beginning of the change process and listening, these parents may revert to guilt and shame.

It does not help to wallow in guilt. This often compounds the problem by inviting children to feel it is their job to make parents feel better. Guilt is often used as an excuse to avoid change. It is normal for people in recovery to feel guilt and shame. The most effective way to deal with guilt and shame is to use emotional honesty to express those feelings, apologize, and then focus on solutions for now and the future. The following story about Erik's family illustrates the unhealthy patterns created when we don't use emotional honesty.

Erik was an alcoholic. He used alcohol to mask his feelings instead of being honest about them. When Erik was sober, he'd say he would do something and get the kids' hopes up. Then he'd start drinking and forget to follow through.

When the kids expressed hurt and disappointment (emotional honesty) over the broken promises, Erik attacked and yelled at them, telling them they were ungrateful and demanding. Instead of being able to have their feelings and express them, the kids went underground with their hurt feelings by refusing to talk to their father (emotional dishonesty). They did not trust Erik and refused to be close to him.

Erik reacted to their rejection by pounding his fists on the table and criticizing them without mercy. The kids would start to cry, and Erik would send them to their rooms for "acting like babies."

In Erik's family, as in most families plagued by addiction, it wasn't OK for anyone to be emotionally honest. And Erik was teaching his kids to repeat his unhealthy communication patterns. The kids weren't encouraged to express their feelings. Their thoughts, questions, and ideas weren't treated with dignity and respect.

The dishonesty was compounded because Erik had adopted the conventional wisdom about mistakes and thought he was a bad parent because of his mistakes. He didn't know that it is OK to make mistakes and that it is never too late to heal. Erik kept trying to cover up mistakes (dishonesty) instead of admitting that he made them (honesty).

Using Emotional Honesty to Heal the Past

The growth process began the day Erik admitted he was an alcoholic and was powerless over alcohol. This was his first step in the process of emotional honesty. Erik stopped drinking and started attending AA meetings.

Erik became clean and sober, but nothing changed with his kids. Even though it was extremely painful to face the truth, Erik realized he had a horrible relationship with his kids. This was another step in emotional honesty that made it possible for Erik to start the process of rebuilding trust with his kids, even though he wasn't quite sure where to begin.

Beginning the Change Process

Erik found a support group that helped him get in touch with feelings and have the courage to express them with emotional honesty. This was not easy for Erik, because emotional dishonesty was a way of life for him. He had never learned anything else. He was out of touch with his feelings, as were the other members of his family. They all thought their survival depended on not talking, feeling, or trusting.

It was hard not to go back to old patterns, but Erik told himself, "It will get better and it's not too late." He realized he had to *work his twelve-step program* and practice emotional honesty every day if he wanted to rebuild trust with his kids.

The group leader reminded Erik that becoming aware that he had a poor relationship with his kids and wanting to learn new skills was the first step to making things better. She encouraged him to compliment himself on the progress he was making, instead of emotionally beating himself up for not turning things around immediately with his kids. It was only natural that it would take time—Erik's kids had been deeply hurt and wanted to hurt him back.

Erik discovered the hard way that his group leader was right. He kept hoping things would change quickly, but when he tried to get close to his kids and be part of their lives, the kids didn't want to tell him anything. When he asked questions, they were silent or they antagonized him and tried to get him to explode. They tried to push his guilt buttons with statements like, "You never cared before. Why should we care now?" If he did explode and react with anger, they ran to their rooms shouting, "We hate you," and slammed their doors.

Erik's kids weren't unusual. They had lived so long with mistrust that they needed time to know they could trust their father or trust their own feelings and express them. Hurt, anger, and loneliness were more familiar to them.

Children in a family plagued by addiction spend much time being alone, or feeling alone even when others are around. For obvious reasons, the parent addicted to drugs isn't available as a nurturing parent. What is not so obvious is that even in a two-parent family the children are still lonely because the nonaddicted parent usually is too caught up in co-dependent behaviors to be a nurturing parent. Co-dependent parents spend most of their time focusing on the addict instead of the kids.

Moving from guilt and shame to emotional honesty, one step at a time, is a process, not an event. Erik's support group continued to give him the encouragement he needed to keep trusting the process of emotional honesty, even through the difficult times.

Reviewing the Process of Emotional Honesty

As we see in the preceding example, the first thing Erik learned was how to identify his feelings. Most people can tell others what they *think*, but have a difficult time telling how they *feel*. They are too busy evaluating, judging, rationalizing, and comparing. These are activities of the thought domain, not the feeling domain.

Feelings are different from thoughts. Feelings describe something that is going on inside each person. When you learn to tap into those feelings, you gain a wealth of information about yourself. Feelings aren't good or bad, right or wrong, proper or improper, logical or illogical. They are just feelings.

Many people struggle when they first try expressing feelings. They use statements that include the words *like, that, as if, you,* or *they,* following the word *feel.* These words indicate that the speaker is talking about thoughts, not feelings. For example, the remark "I feel like I can't do anything right" is a thought not a feeling. The comment, "I feel discouraged," expresses a feeling about not being about to do anything right. With few exceptions, any time you use more than one word after *feel* you are expressing thoughts not feelings. It takes practice to become aware of and express feelings.

Most people find it helpful to know that feelings can usually be described with one word. A few examples of feeling words are *happy, hurt, comfortable, scared, hungry, sleepy, angry, sad, helpless, hopeless, irritated, embarrassed, ashamed,* and *joyful.* When you find yourself trying to use more than one word to describe a feeling, you can slow your thought process down and move into the feeling domain by searching for the *one* word that describes your feeling. Also, it helps to know that just because you identify and feel your feelings, that doesn't mean you have to *do* anything you don't want to do. The most important steps are to notice the feeling, give it a name, and tell others how you feel.

Erik Practices Emotional Honesty

Erik thought he was talking about his feelings when he used the word *like.* For example, he would say to the kids, "I feel like I've been rejected."

Erik learned to ask himself instead, "How does it make me feel when I think I have been rejected? Do I feel hurt, angry, scared, or worthless?" Then Erik would practice the new sentence with his kids: "I feel hurt when you run into your room saying you hate me. I wish we could talk about things instead of yelling and hurting each other. I know I used to do that to you, and I'm sorry. I wish we could try again so we can learn new ways to be with each other."

Sometimes Erik's kids would say, "It's OK, Dad. We were just mad." At other times they would stay in their room for a while with the door shut, but for the rest of the day they would be friendly with Erik. It was hard for them to hang on to their revengeful behavior when Erik shared his feelings with them, being emotionally honest.

Another part of emotional honesty that helped Erik was learning the difference between feelings and actions. The feeling of anger is very different from a display of anger. Many people have buried their feelings of anger because of the mistaken notion that feeling angry and acting angry is the same. A display of anger usually includes irrational behavior like yelling, screaming, judging, or blaming others.

Expressing anger is simply saying, "I feel angry about what happened." This can be said with dignity and respect for yourself and for the other person. It is usually best to wait until you have calmed down to "do" anything.

Erik remembered how often he used a display of anger to cover up his true feelings of shame for disappointing the kids with his broken promises. Sometimes, he admitted, he yelled at his kids and pretended he was angry, even when he wasn't. He mistakenly believed a display of anger was a good way to make them do better. Other times Erik pretended he wasn't angry when he was. He held his anger inside and hoped someone would guess how bad he was feeling. Erik learned that no one could really know how he was feeling inside unless he told them.

As he continued practicing emotional honesty, it became easier. When he realized he had feelings, he gave them a name and then told others how he felt. Erik learned to say what he was thinking. If it was on his mind, he put it on his lips. His children responded with more acceptance and forgiveness. They learned, by Erik's example, to share their own feelings. They all felt more closeness and trust through identifying and sharing their feelings without judgment. Erik and his kids had begun the process of mending broken trust through emotional honesty.

So emotional honesty requires identifying feelings, giving them a name, and learning to share them without judgment. Just because you decide to be emotionally honest doesn't mean that it will be easy. You may encounter some problems by being emotionally honest in a dishonest world.

The Dangers of Emotional Honesty

Sometimes you may not feel safe being emotionally honest because you are vulnerable and the people around you are not always good listeners. They may try to talk you out of your feelings or fix them. Others may get defensive and attack when you are emotionally honest.

It is a common mistake for others to believe that when you share your feelings you are making a statement about *them* instead of giving information about yourself. They may think you are talking about them when you say, "I'm really angry at you." What you are really saying is, "I feel anger, which is inside of me, about something you have done." You are talking about your own anger. If people you are talking to get defensive, they may attack or shut down instead of being curious about your anger. Expressing your feelings is still worth the risk, for without emotional honesty there is little self-acceptance, acceptance of others, or growth.

When people react by trying to correct your feelings or defend themselves, you can be ready to tell them, "I just want you to hear me. You don't have to fix me, defend yourself, or agree with me." Also, you can watch your tendencies to defend or fix others.

Emotional honesty works two ways. You are emotionally honest when you express your feelings, and you are emotionally honest when you listen to other people's feelings. You can be better listeners when you know and avoid the blocks to emotional honesty.

Blocks to Emotional Honesty

There are five major ways in which people tend to block emotional honesty.

1. Trying to fix things, explaining, or defending instead of listening
2. Ignoring, withdrawing, changing the subject, or telling people to mind their own business
3. Using nonverbal blocks such as tone of voice and body language that show judgment or defensiveness
4. Giving mixed messages by saying one thing and doing the opposite
5. Forgetting that people expressing feelings are sharing information about themselves, not you

Erik's support group leader presented information on the blocks to emotional honesty. Dirk, a member of Erik's support group, shared with the group, "I use all the blocks to emotional honesty. I try to fix situations by apologizing for my feelings. I tell people to mind their own business, and I ignore situations by withdrawing or changing the subject."

Dirk realized, as he continued to listen to the presentation, that he also communicated nonverbally in ways that blocked emotional honesty. He had a sharp tone in his voice when he spoke to his son. He would square his shoulders, furrow his brow, and stand with his hands on his hips. He remembered that day his 10-year-old son, Andy, had asked him, "Dad, why do you make your lips so tight?" Dirk hadn't realized how much he communicated nonverbally.

When he went home that evening, Dirk noticed he also gave mixed messages that were confusing. First, he told his son it's not OK to yell. Then, when Laura, his ex-wife, called to cancel a date with Andy, Dirk yelled and slammed the phone down. Dirk told Andy he should respect his mother and love her, yet he was always angry and disrespectful when he talked to or about his ex-wife. Dirk's double messages put Andy in a bind. If Andy showed love for his mother, he was afraid it would upset his father, but he didn't want to hurt his mother's feelings by acting mean and hostile, as his father did.

Dirk had reasons for his anger. Laura was a cocaine addict, and her addiction made it extremely difficult to work anything out. Dirk often had feelings of extreme frustration and anger after talking with Laura.

One day while Dirk was on the phone with Laura, Andy overheard his father arguing with his mother. He got very angry and said to his father, "Don't talk that way to my mother!" When Dirk heard Andy yell at him, he realized this was an opportunity to practice what he was learning in his group. When Dirk got off the phone, he explained to Andy, "Sometimes people get angry and argue. It is OK to have those feelings. The arguing is between your mother and me and is not about you. Would you like to share with me how it makes you feel when you hear me argue with your mother?"

Andy: I don't like it. I don't like you to be mean to my mom.

Dirk (letting Andy know he heard him): When you think I'm being mean to your mother, you don't like it.

Andy: Yeah!

Dirk (realizing Andy didn't know how to express his feelings): I appreciate what you think. Could I make some guesses about feelings you might be having?

Andy: Yeah.

Dirk: Does it hurt your feelings when you think someone is hurting your mom?

Andy: Yeah.

Dirk: Do you feel angry when someone hurts your mom?

Andy: Yeah.

Dirk: Do you feel protective of your mom?

Andy: Yeah.

Andy couldn't acknowledge and name his feelings without Dirk's help because he hadn't learned to recognize and understand his feelings. Dirk wanted to help Andy understand his feelings and accept them without judgment. He also wanted to help Andy learn the difference between feelings and actions.

Teaching the Difference Between Feelings and Actions

Dirk continued the conversation by acknowledging Andy's feelings: "You have many feelings around your mother. You feel hurt, angry, and protective. Your feelings are very normal. What you decide to do is very different from what you feel. You decided to tell me you don't like it. That is a very healthy thing to do. What else would you like to do?"

Andy answered, "I want you to stop arguing with my mom."

Dirk said, "That is what you want me to do, and it is a good idea. I need to work on that, but I can't promise you I will do it. This is another good thing for you to learn. We can't control what others do. We can control only what we do. Can you think of something else you could do?"

Andy replied, "Yeah. I don't like to listen to it, so I'll just leave the room."

Dirk said, "I really appreciate you taking care of yourself and letting me take care of myself. That is very respectful. We can both learn a lot about accepting our feelings and then making decisions about what we can do."

Emotional Honesty Leads to Self-Respect, Closeness, and Trust

Dirk and Andy continued to practice noticing their feelings, naming them, and sharing them. This built trust and closeness, and the healing continued.

Dirk was surprised and pleased with their progress. One night he told the rest of the group, "In the past, when I felt bad about myself, I tried to hide. I alternated between guilt and blame and wanted everyone else to change. I did not have a good relationship with my son, and I was very lonely. I was afraid if I said how I really felt, it would make things worse. I felt hopeless and helpless. It seems ironic that telling the truth can be so powerful."

Erik and Dirk learned that their feelings of personal worth and connection with others grew in direct proportion to their practice of emotional honesty. Practicing openness and self-disclosure improved their recovery and their relationships with their kids.

The more parents practice emotional honesty, saying what they mean and meaning what they say, the more kids can trust them. Negative experience over time creates distrust. Positive experience over time creates trust, *even when there has been a history of distrust.* Children change as you change. They do need time and guidance. They have many feelings from the past, and the more you can help them identify, name, and express those feelings, the more progress you make.

Through emotional honesty, you can learn to know and accept yourself. As you accept yourself, it is easier to be accepting of others. You can give and take feedback without judgment. You can help each other without comparing and competing. You can learn to listen and share with emotional honesty. You can feel close to others, and your children can become trusting of you. It's worth the risk.

Chapter

3

Connect with Outside Support Groups

When you take care of yourself and become healthy, whole people, you can be better models for your children. Effective parenting includes effective self-parenting. One of the most effective ways you can care for yourself in recovery is to connect with outside support groups. In support groups, you can learn and grow while you are helping your kids learn and grow. It is much easier to grow and change with the help of support groups than to try to "go it alone." In support groups, you have the encouragement of others, learn from others, see that others have similar problems, know you are not alone, and have the opportunity to help others (in ways that do not foster dependency).

Support Groups Help You Help Others in Ways That Do Not Foster Dependency

Have you ever noticed how easy it is to solve *other* people's problems? Their mistakes seem obvious. You can be objective and rational, can see their lives with perspective. From your position, you can give suggestions and helpful encouragement. And others can do the same for you. We all learn to be valuable consultants for each other. Helping others is an important step to self-healing.

Alfred Adler, a renowned psychiatrist, taught that the key to mental health is social interest, the ability to care about others, contribute and connect with others. Support groups provide ample opportunities to practice social interest in ways that do not foster dependency.

Mistaken Notions About Therapy and Support Groups

Too many people avoid therapy and support groups because they believe they should be able to handle all their own problems. They believe that seeking help is an admission something is wrong with them. We, however, see therapy as an educational process where people can learn to improve their lives. Therapists and other group members can act as coaches to help people see the things they can't see and give them suggestions for improvement. (All champions look for good teams and good coaches.)

We all have room for improvement. In that sense, there *is* something "wrong" or lacking in each one of us. But that isn't bad. All people lack something before they learn to read and write. People seek education to correct those deficiencies. People never become perfect. Education, growth, and change are a lifelong process and an important part of recovery.

Many recovering addicts and their significant others find twelve-step groups extremely helpful for growth and change. Some believe twelve-step groups are the only outside support groups people in recovery should attend. We (the authors) recommend any combination of activities and groups that enrich and encourage people to live healthier, more productive lives. When children are involved, it is not appropriate to compound their pain by choosing a recovery program that neglects their needs. Twelve-step programs do not focus specifically on family issues, but on individual recovery.

Parenting is one area where many people have believed they can do an effective job without support and education. Some have been successful, but most people benefit from attending support groups to learn parenting skills. As we emphasized so strongly in the Introduction to this book, parents in recovery can use parenting support groups to learn skills to overcome the guilt and pain of neglecting or abusing their children in the past.

Parenting Classes Offer Options for Dealing with Guilt and Shame

Parents can actually strengthen their recovery when they learn new skills to deal effectively with their children in the present. Too many parents sabotage their recovery process when they use ineffective parenting techniques. Some believe spoiling their kids helps make up for past neglect. Then they feel resentful and frustrated when their kids behave like spoiled brats. Other parents become so involved in their personal recovery that they neglect their kids as much as they did when they were abusing chemicals. Some parents in recovery are reluctant to start a parenting class because they are ashamed and believe they are the only ones with problems.

You Are Not Alone

Sheila's therapist urged her to take a parenting class. She agreed, but felt scared and vulnerable. She believed she would be the only parent with such severe problems. She was sure everyone would judge and criticize her for what she believed were her "many stupid mistakes." At the first group meeting, Sheila decided to listen and not say anything.

One member of the group, Betty, shared an incident in which her alcoholic husband verbally attacked one of their children. She asked for help in figuring out how to handle this problem when it came up again. The group role-played the situation and brainstormed alternatives, and Betty chose the suggestion she wanted to try. Sheila watched in amazement. The problem was so similar to her problem.

The next group member, Burt, told how his ex-wife showed up drunk for her day with the kids. He refused to let the kids get into the car with her, and she started an ugly scene in front of the neighbors and the kids. The group members gave several suggestions for Burt to try. Although Sheila had not said a word, she herself decided to try one of the suggestions listed for Burt. Several weeks later she shared the following story in her parenting class:

> I was sure I was the only person who had these problems. I used to have ugly scenes with my ex-husband, when he would show up drunk on his day with the kids. I followed a suggestion I heard here

a few weeks ago, to honor my common sense, to take a stand on what I am willing to do with dignity and respect, and to teach my kids to do the same. I told my ex-husband, "I taught the kids about personal safety and self-respect. From now on we can meet at McDonald's on your day with the kids. I will wait in the parking lot. If the kids are afraid to ride in your car because they smell alcohol or think you are drunk, they can get back in the car with me. If they refuse to go with you, you can try again the following week." I think he could tell I meant it. He had never seen me take a stand with such firmness and confidence, yet lacking in blame or judgment. We haven't had an ugly scene for three weeks.

Sheila's feelings of shame turned to feelings of eagerness and curiosity. She was no longer silent in her parenting group, and she found she had suggestions to offer during the brainstorming time. She discovered how easy it is to get perspective on other people's problems. And she felt comfortable giving and receiving suggestions, because the group did not use judgments and criticisms. Instead, they focused on offering solutions and giving unconditional love.

Sheila felt empowered through her improved parenting skills. Her skills helped her kids feel empowered, too. The family was able to significantly reduce the cycle of discouragement created by their experience with substance abuse.

Parent Education Can Break the Discouraging Patterns Created by Abuse

In Judy's family, the substance of abuse was religion instead of chemicals. Judy describes her parents as "church-a-holics." She did not feel empowered by her parents to think for herself. Her parents believed it was their job to tell Judy what was "right" and make sure she did it. She grew up with low self-esteem and often believed she was "bad" when she didn't do the "right" thing. When Judy had children, she found herself following the example set by her parents, though she hated it.

When Judy repeated the patterns she learned from her parents, she started getting the same results—open rebellion from one child, passive resistance from another, and sneakiness from her youngest child. She knew that what she was doing with her kids wasn't working, and she wanted to change her patterns.

Judy became an avid reader of parenting books and attended many parenting groups. Her relationship with her three kids improved dramatically. They held regular family meetings and gave each other compliments. The kids helped with chores, and were cooperative most of the time. Judy eventually became a parent-group leader because she wanted to share with others the skills that had helped her so much.

Then Matt, her teenage son, started using chemicals, stealing, and cutting school. Judy panicked, and returned to the controlling and rescuing techniques she had learned from her parents. She felt this problem was too serious for the respectful methods she had been learning and teaching and that it was her duty to "make" Matt be good.

She tried punishment by grounding Matt and withdrawing privileges. Matt rebelled even more. Eventually, Matt got kicked out of school and spent most of his time with his friends drinking and drugging. The first time Matt went to juvenile hall, Judy rescued him by hiring an attorney to get him out. She was furious with Matt. She gave him a thorough tongue lashing and increased her controlling, punishing methods. (Instead of changing their behavior, parents often revert to old patterns when something doesn't work.)

Then Matt got picked up by the police again. This was a turning point for Judy. She knew she needed help. She went back to a parenting class and received the kind of support and encouragement she needed. The group helped her realize that Matt needed to experience the consequences of his behavior and that if she bailed him out, things would only get worse.

Instead of bailing Matt out of juvenile hall, Judy provided him with a choice. Judy convinced the juvenile authorities that Matt's problems stemmed from his abuse of chemicals and that a treatment program would be more helpful than thirty days in juvenile hall. They agreed, and gave Matt the choice of a treatment program or jail.

Matt tried to get Judy to feel sorry for him and rescue him, but she remained kind and firm. She told him the decision was his and that she would come visit him and bring him cookies if he chose jail. If he chose the treatment program, she would work out the financial arrangements, but they would not take him unless it was his decision and unless he called them to verbalize his commitment.

It was scary for Judy to let Matt experience the consequences of his choices. Sometimes she felt guilty that she was unable to "make" him do the "right" things all the time. It was a major change in attitude for her to realize that Matt had a right to control his life. She knew that empowering Matt sometimes meant doing what was hardest for her in the short term (such as not fixing or trying to control) but better for him in the long term (such as experiencing the consequences of his choices).

Matt chose a treatment program in another state, and after treatment chose a halfway house away from his old friends. For Judy, choosing to be an empowering parent instead of a rescuing, critical parent was like lancing a festering boil. It was painful at first, but Matt got the help he needed and began to take responsibility for his life. Matt later said he felt more love and respect when his mother didn't rescue him than when she did. He also knew he had to think about his choices and the consequences of his choices when he was on his own.

Judy did not abandon Matt when she quit trying to control him. She turned into an active parent instead of a reactive parent. She actively helped provide a choice for Matt. She actively looked for an after-care program that would be beneficial to Matt. And she actively let him know how much she loved him, and would love him no matter what he chose. Judy's parenting group helped her change old patterns and beliefs as well as gave her the opportunity to practice new skills.

We can't emphasize enough how important it is for recovering parents to attend parenting classes to improve family relationships. We recommend attending other support groups, for additional personal growth. Most people in recovery are familiar with the benefits of twelve-step groups. We also want to point out the benefits of attending other groups in order to enhance the recovery process.

Group Members Call Us on Our Mischief and Support Us in Making Healthy Changes

Mischief is any behavior or thinking that is useless or unproductive in the recovery process. Some support groups give members the opportunity to interact in a social setting and to let others see them and give non-judgmental feedback.

Natalie, a single parent, never had time for herself. She was trying to work on her problems, find time for her kids, attend support group meetings, spend time with her sponsor in the twelve-step program, work her steps, read, meditate, write, and work full time. Her parents and family voiced criticism of how much time she spent away from the kids. Natalie felt guilty when others said, "Why do you have to go to those meetings? You should be home with the kids." She felt overwhelmed and wondered why she quit drinking in the first place.

As part of her recovery, Natalie needed time for herself and for personal growth. Her sponsor and her therapist encouraged her to ignore criticism by others and to take time for healing herself first. They explained that she would have more to give once she felt healthier and had more self-esteem.

Natalie joined two groups—a parenting class and a twelve-step group. These two groups helped her find the balance she needed in her life to take care of herself and her kids. Attending the twelve-step group helped Natalie feel secure in caring for herself. Listening to others helped her see how her guilt turned to anger when she didn't take care of herself. She could see that wasn't helping anyone. Her habit of responding to her family's opinions of what she "should" do had stopped her from seeing what she *wanted* to do.

Natalie's parenting class helped her see how much of her time with her children was not helpful to them. She was too overcontrolling. Instead of teaching her kids to be responsible, she thought it was her job to stick her nose in everyone's business and make sure they did what they were supposed to do. No wonder she felt overwhelmed and frustrated. It was actually helpful for Natalie and her kids when she went to meetings instead of thinking she had to do everything. She became a better parent by teaching her kids more skills to handle things while she was at meetings.

Natalie started family meetings with her children so they all could be involved in solving problems. The kids were more responsible in following through with plans when they were involved in creating them. They also planned for family fun time, which helped them enjoy each other and feel closer as a family. Natalie stopped worrying about the opinions and criticisms of others when she felt confident about what she was doing. She was helping herself and her kids grow and change.

Support groups can help us give up our co-dependence. Before Natalie learned this, most of the time she spent with her family was in co-dependent interactions. When all family members join a support group, they can all learn to stop co-dependent behaviors and get individual help.

Family Members Learn About Chemical Abuse and Get Help for Themselves in Support Groups

It is amazing how much misinformation and lack of information family members have about dependence and co-dependence. Groups offer the kind of information and support that can help us give up these patterns, that can help us learn healthy patterns of relating that promote healing and growth.

Nina did not know what co-dependency was until she got into a support group and learned she was a co-dependent. Jack and Nina had two young children under the age of 5 and another one on the way. Jack was using both alcohol and cocaine.

A turning point for Nina was the time Jack went on a binge and didn't come home for four days. He attempted suicide during that time. When Nina picked him up at the hospital, she confronted him: "Jack, get help or you'll never see me or the kids again." When she confronted Jack, she thought he was the only one who needed help.

Jack checked into a drug treatment program. The family therapist called Nina for an interview and explained that Nina was playing a part in Jack's drug use. She gave Nina information about the groups available for family members.

Nina was shocked and angry. She saw this as Jack's problem and thought she herself was the victim. She had not heard the terms *co-dependent* or *enabling* before. Co-dependents are people who are focused on what they think others *should* do instead of on what they *will* or *won't* do. Enabling is behaving in ways that minimize the consequences of other people's behavior through rescuing or other interference. This stops the rescued people from growing and learning from their choices.

Nina was willing to go to the groups, but she still told herself it was to help Jack. Once she was there, she got a picture of what enabling was all about. Every story she heard could have been about her. She realized that enabling was like trying to put out a fire with gasoline. She could see that her attempts to rescue Jack or nag at him not only didn't help, but made things worse. Nina said, "My education started then. I stopped focusing on my husband's behavior and focused on my own."

In fact, it's not just the drug abuser and his or her co-dependent partner who need support groups. Rather, drug abuse affects everyone in a family in different ways. Therefore, it is important to get everyone, including the kids, involved in support groups if they are available.

Kids Find Encouragement and Empowerment in Groups

Kids' groups can provide a safe space where kids can talk about what's been happening in their families and learn that it wasn't their fault. Kids also can learn about their feelings and how to share them. They need to know, just as the adults do, that they aren't alone and that other kids have similar problems.

Jerry Moe and Don Pohlman wrote a beautiful book called *Kids' Power: Healing Games for Children of Alcoholics*. In that book, they present games and activities to help children heal. They remind us how important it is for kids from alcoholic homes to remember the four C's and the five S's.

The Four C's

I didn't CAUSE the alcoholism.

I can't CONTROL it.

I can't CURE it.

But I can learn how to COPE with it.

The Five S's

I didn't START the alcoholism.

I can't STOP it.

I don't have to SUFFER with it.

I don't have to feel SHAME because of it.

I can SAVE myself in spite of it.[1]

---

[1] Jerry Moe and Don Pohlman, *Kids' Power: Healing Games for Children of Alcoholics* (Deerfield Beach, FL: Health Communications, 1989).

It is important that groups for children empower them so they can learn more skills that make their lives work, even when they can't count on their parents. Effective groups focus on helping children to get in touch with their uniqueness and to know they are worthwhile people.

It is important for kids to get accurate information about drug addiction. Many children living in homes where a parent is abusing chemicals think they themselves are bad when their parents act crazy. They don't understand what chemical dependency is or how it can affect people.

In a kids' group, they can find out that it was normal to think of their family as different and that they were not being disloyal when they felt ashamed of their family. It was normal to want to hide their differences from their friends.

Kids are good *observers*, but not necessarily accurate *interpreters* of what they see happening around them. They often make poor decisions about themselves, life, and others, based on their faulty interpretations. The following three adult children of alcoholics tell their stories about the mistaken decisions they made as children. If they as children had attended a group, they might have formed more realistic pictures of what was happening around them.

When Katy was six, her father was an alcoholic. When he drank, he drove himself and Katy to bars, where he would show her off and buy her candy and vodka for himself. Then he would take her out and buy her a new outfit. When they came home, Katy's mom would yell at her husband for wasting money on frilly dresses instead of school clothes. Katy hated her mother for being so nasty when she and her dad were having so much fun. She didn't realize her father was an alcoholic. She decided he was the good guy and her mom, the bad guy.

In another family, Vanessa watched her father get drunk and fall asleep in his chair every night. Vanessa's mother insisted his strange behavior was caused by his blood pressure medicine, not by the vodka he drank. Vanessa was embarrassed and confused. She decided she couldn't trust her instincts. She also decided men were useless.

When Victor was a teenager, he watched his father cash his paycheck, go to the local bar for a few drinks, and then call his mom to join him. When they came home, his mom was crying. Dad pulled his clothes out of drawers and threw them into his truck, threatening to move out. Victor knew his parents had been drinking. As he watched his parents repeat this scene every Friday night, he decided marriage—not alcohol—was a bad idea. He vowed that he'd never get married and that he'd leave home as soon as possible to look for a different kind of life.

Katy, Vanessa, and Victor were typical of children who are good observers but who don't understand the part alcohol plays in their families. They formed faulty conclusions about how to survive because they lacked information and understanding of what was happening. Kids' groups can teach children about chemical abuse so they can change their conclusions.

Group Support Helps Break the Cycle of Alcoholism and Invites People into Recovery

We've talked about how, after getting into recovery, people can use groups for support to enhance the recovery process. We've also shown how nonusing co-dependent family members find help through group support. Some people, like Carla in the next example, also use group support to help themselves get *into* recovery.

Carla's friend Betsy, a recovering alcoholic, told Carla about some of the ways she'd behaved when she was drinking. The behavior that caught Carla's attention was topping off drinks when no one was looking: Carla had been doing that herself.

Carla wondered, "Could I be an alcoholic?" Until she listened to Betsy describe her symptoms, the possibility had never occurred to her. Carla realized she was doing many of the things Betsy described. Her sneaky behavior included hiding how much she was drinking by tearing up the boxes of wine before putting them in the garbage or topping off her drinks in the kitchen when she was entertaining, so no one could see how much she had had to drink.

The next week Carla hosted a bridge party and drank all day long. Nobody knew she was drunk, but late that night she was exceptionally mean to her husband *for no apparent reason.* She had a flashback of her alcoholic dad being mean to her mom and realized she was acting like her dad.

The next morning after her husband went to work, Carla decided she wanted to apologize to him. She dropped her son off at school and started heading to her husband's work site sixty miles away. But she couldn't keep the car in her lane. People were honking at her, and she realized she was still drunk from the day before. She wondered how she could be sober and drunk simultaneously.

Carla knew Betsy could answer her questions. They went to lunch, and Carla told Betsy what had happened. The fact that she was still drunk the next day indicated a serious problem. Betsy knew it was time to share more of her story with Carla.

Betsy said she knew she had a problem when she hid bottles in the cupboard. When her kids wanted to go to McDonald's, Betsy said no, because they didn't serve wine. Carla thought, "I do that."

Betsy continued, "It is up to you to decide if you are an alcoholic. I have shared with you some of the signs I was willing to recognize. Alcoholism is like being on an elevator going down. You can get off at any floor. You don't have to wait till the bottom floor, but once you are on the elevator you need outside help to recover." This was a turning point for Carla. She was scared by her behavior. She knew she didn't want to be like her alcoholic father, so she accepted Betsy's invitation to go to an AA meeting.

At the AA meeting, Carla found it extremely encouraging to listen to others who were dealing with similar situations. Being around other people who had been practicing sobriety for a long time helped Carla learn new patterns. She found hope in the knowledge that it was not too late for her and that she could get better. She would not have to go through life as an active alcoholic like her father. Carla decided to continue attending AA meetings and to start her recovery program. When a person is toying with the idea of getting into recovery, attending an already existing support group may be the move that gets him or her into recovery. As for Carla, the group helps them end their isolation and offers hope.

Support Groups Help End the Isolation of Chemical Dependency and Remind You That You Are Not Alone

Addicts and their families live in an isolated world. They have so many secrets to keep, because they feel a misguided sense of loyalty to protect the family. To overcome these destructive and isolating patterns, family members can connect with outside support groups during recovery instead of trying to do it alone.

Carla started to notice how many people were alcoholics and in denial because of their lack of information. They were abusing chemicals, and no one said anything about it. She realized that if she had continued without help, her husband would not have said anything, but most likely would have left her. He had left his previous wife because of her drinking. He never dealt honestly with her alcoholism—he just left.

Carla realized she had behaved in similar ways. Before going to AA, Carla often spent a lot of time drinking, to hide out. And often she dealt with her son while she was in an alcoholic fog. Before she had support, Carla felt guilty and ashamed that she had abandoned her son. But in her support groups, she realized that she wasn't alone and that she could change.

As Carla learned more about the problems of alcoholism, she had the courage to find other support groups to help her learn new skills. A parenting group helped her learn new ways to interact with her son.

Now, when her son is home, Carla makes sure she spends special time with him, listening to stories about his day. Her son is grateful for the attention. It used to hurt his feelings when he came home, called, "Hello," and no one answered. Now, instead of feeling lonely and abandoned he knows his mother cares about him.

Carla remembered a Christmas party where everyone was singing carols and she was high. She had had a lot to drink and was grumpy and snappy with her son. When he complained that she was singing "really weird," she said, "Don't bother me! Leave me alone, I don't want to deal with you!" Now that she is sober and dealing with her feelings she is much more patient and understanding with her son. She has her sense of humor back and doesn't feel so defensive. She said, "Now, if my son said I was singing weird, I'd say, 'Yeah, I sure am.'"

Carla learned that giving up drinking is not enough for an effective recovery program. She also needed life-changing skills. One reason why problems are not solved when someone in a chemically dependent family stops using is that giving up chemical use doesn't change the compulsions of the mind or the patterns within the family. Being in a dry drunk means continuing the thinking, feelings, and behaviors of an addict after chemical abuse has stopped.

Support Groups Help Break the "Dry Drunk" Cycle

If people don't change how they think, feel, or behave, they'll keep getting poor results in their lives. A support group can provide opportunities to process and change thoughts, feelings, and actions through feedback and information.

Ernie, for example, stopped and started using alcohol for over nine years. Then he switched to other drugs as a way of giving up alcohol. When he realized that wasn't working, he decided he needed help. He started attending AA meetings, but soon decided that he was different and didn't need the meetings to stop using drugs.

This time he was successful. He completely stopped using drugs and alcohol. However, his behavior didn't change. He was angry and resentful most of the time. Ernie saw himself acting like his alcoholic father. Like his father, he'd yell and criticize the kids until they cried. He thought if they felt bad enough they would change. It had never worked for him when he was a kid, though, and it wasn't working with his kids. His family didn't trust him, because he wasn't there for them. He didn't finish things he agreed to do. He would build up people's hopes and then not follow through. In his words, "I couldn't even take care of myself and keep any kind of balance, so how could I possibly or honestly be there for someone else's needs?"

Ernie remembered a discussion about being "in a dry drunk" and realized he fit the description. He had quit chemicals but nothing else had changed. He had stopped chemical abuse on his own, but he realized he needed outside help to change his behaviors. This time he stuck with his AA meetings, got a sponsor, worked on his twelve-step program, and got into a parenting group.

Ernie found that because he experienced so much isolation, denial, helplessness, and hopelessness even after he stopped using, it was especially important for him to reach out. In his support groups, Ernie could share his feelings and his problems. No one told him he was doing it wrong or criticized him. For Ernie, as for many others, sharing his experience aloud in front of others was the first step out of isolation and hopelessness.

Through his work in his parenting group, Ernie is learning how to listen to his kids. Now he talks with them instead of yelling at them. And because overpromising was a big problem for him, he is focusing on following through. He knows it will take time, but he can already feel increased trust from his kids.

Ernie felt tremendous relief to discover that information and skills could make such a difference in his life. Before he joined his support groups, he was beginning to believe he was just a bad person who couldn't trust himself. Now he knows better.

Support Groups Provide Validation to Help Us Know We Can Trust Our Inner Wisdom

Members of a support group don't have an interest in keeping us dependent, as co-dependent family members may, so their feedback is more honest and objective. Sometimes we need validation from others to get a reality check. They can encourage us to trust our inner wisdom.

Harry and Jennifer had been married five years when Harry started meeting Eva after work for a quick drink. He and Eva drank, laughed, and flirted with each other for hours. When Jennifer asked if she could join them, Harry explained they were talking business and it would be boring for her. He reminded Jennifer her first responsibility was to the toddlers at home, and their budget didn't cover extra money for baby-sitting.

Jennifer kept questioning Harry, asking if his relationship with Eva was more than business. Harry told Jennifer she was suspicious and mean to suggest such a thing. He reminded Jennifer how important she and the babies were to him and scolded her for doubting his word.

Jennifer felt troubled but was afraid to talk about this problem with anyone. She didn't want anyone to think badly of Harry or think she wasn't a good wife. One day, her neighbor came by for coffee and found Jennifer red-nosed and teary-eyed at the kitchen table. She encouraged Jennifer to tell her what was wrong. Jennifer told her the story, even though she kept saying throughout, "I must be crazy to be so suspicious. Harry tells me I'm overly concerned. I feel jealous and scared, and Harry tells me I'm just being a baby."

Her neighbor invited Jennifer to attend her women's support group with her that evening. When Jennifer protested that she needed to stay home with the kids, her neighbor convinced her it was important enough for her to get a sitter.

At the group, Jennifer heard similar stories and had the courage to share hers. A woman in the group said, "If anyone treated me that way, I would tell him I love myself too much to be treated so dishonestly. If he continued to put another relationship before ours, that is his problem, but he could move out until he thought our relationship was worth the effort."

Jennifer felt validated and started to cry. She said, "I can't believe you could say that. It's what I want to say, but I keep doubting myself. Now I know I'm not crazy. I have been denying my inner voice that told me I was being a fool."

Group support gave Jennifer the courage to deal with her husband without backing down. She told him it was not OK for him to spend time with another woman if he wanted to be married to her. She stuck up for herself by saying, "I know I'm not crazy to feel hurt about this. I know you wouldn't like it if I spent time at a bar drinking with another man while you were home with the kids."

At first Harry was angry, and threatened to leave. Then he told her to leave if she was going to act like a suspicious, jealous wife. Jennifer replied, "I can't see any reason I should leave our house and children when you are the one who is doing something that could break up the marriage. The decision is yours."

Harry slept in the guest room for a week, but Jennifer noticed he came home every night right after work. She told him how much she appreciated having him around. When Harry moved back into their bedroom, Jennifer told her group, "Our relationship still isn't as good as I would like, but at least I stand up for myself when he treats me disrespectfully."

If Jennifer stays in her support group, she will continue to get a reality check on her feelings and thoughts that can help her avoid relapsing into co-dependent behaviors.

Changing Old Patterns and Avoiding Relapse Is Easier in a Support Group

Some people think they are being strong when they keep their problems to themselves and don't "air their dirty laundry in public." The opposite is true. Sharing problems with others takes courage and wisdom. It takes courage to let others see your problems. It takes wisdom to listen to their perspective and suggestions, use what fits for you, and discard what does not fit. Groups can be essential in your process of effective recovery, growth, and change.

It can be tempting to stop growing and improving once the crises are past. Too often people get busy and stop taking care of themselves. But relapses begin when they stop taking care of themselves.

Hank started his recovery program by giving up alcohol and attending AA meetings and a parenting class. He felt proud of himself for his self-improvement and the closeness he was creating with his kids. The only problem was that his many activities created some stress. Six months later, he decided he did not need to attend AA meetings or his parenting class. He was sure he could stay sober and improve his parenting skills without help. Instead of replacing these activities with other helpful activities, however, Hank used his spare time to sit around the house, watch television, and "kick back."

Hank soon relapsed into his old behaviors of yelling at the kids and his wife, though he was still sober. Relapsing is more than an issue of alcohol use. People are relapsing when they engage in self-abuse or behaviors that do not improve their lives.

Hank started to lose respect for himself. He even seriously considered drinking again as a way out. Instead, he went back to his AA meetings and his parenting classes, where he was able to get back into a recovery pattern. His parenting class followed three important guidelines that change addictive patterns and keep people moving forward instead of backward. These guidelines take the form of affirmations:

1. "We created the decisions that motivate our old patterns of behavior, and we can create new decisions to change our behavior."

2. "We are motivated to change when we become aware of behaviors that aren't working and when we stop repeating what doesn't work."

3. "Whatever we practice, we improve. If we practice old behaviors, we will get better at them. With group support, we can practice new decisions and behaviors."

When choosing support groups, it is important to find groups that recognize and practice those three guidelines. In other words, you need to find groups that promote personal responsibility instead of victimization, encourage action instead of explanations, and teach new behaviors for you to practice. Groups that follow these guidelines can help you and give you the opportunity to help others with unconditional love and acceptance.

Support Groups Offer
Unconditional Love and Acceptance

When you know you have worth and surround yourself with others who believe in your worth, you feel loved. When you have faith in yourself and in others, you feel loved. When you are comfortable with who you are in any given moment without judgment, criticism, or ridicule, you feel loved.

It is important to choose a support group that is encouraging and empowering and where participants feel loved unconditionally. With unconditional love, there is no limit to healing and personal growth. As you grow and get healthier, everyone around you benefits.

Support groups that are loving, caring, supportive, and nonjudgmental help break the "don't think, talk, or feel" rules of the chemically dependent family. To move out of the survival, dependency, and crisis state, people need support groups that stimulate courage, responsibility, cooperation, and personal success.

Chapter

4

Break Old Patterns of Co-Dependence

Parents in recovery need a vision of hope to see that their past is not as long as their future. Parents in recovery often say, "I want to do it differently." The vision of hope to change things becomes a reality when we break the patters of co-dependence and encourage independence and interdependence.

Before recovery, you experience the disappointment and destructiveness of dependence and co-dependence. When you learn and teach independence and interdependence, your family becomes a place where people are supported and nurtured, treated with mutual respect, and allowed to grow. In such a family, everyone can start feeling good instead of bad about being in a family.

Dependence—to Independence—to Interdependence

All of us are born dependent. Through the growth process, improved parenting, and the passage of time, we all have the opportunity to become first independent and finally interdependent. Becoming independent (knowing who we are and how to care for ourselves) is the first step toward interdependence (cooperating with others). But too many parents promote dependence and co-dependence instead of independence and interdependence.

Many parents in recovery came from homes where their parents set rules and tried to make the kids follow them. Other parents fixed everything and refused to give their children room to learn from their mistakes and the consequences of their choices. In some homes, the parents were alcoholics or dependent on other drugs and neglected their children. They focused on chemicals as their primary relationship, instead of on their family.

When children are controlled or overprotected or neglected, they do not develop skills for independence and interdependence. They are not encouraged to think for themselves, listen to their feelings, check out their opinions, and value their ideas. They are faced with a set of rules and expectations against which they can rebel or with which they can comply, but they don't learn how to contribute to the family and feel good about themselves. Instead of being encouraged toward independence, children in these families are rewarded for depending on the opinions and guidelines of others. They are punished or shamed if they try to be their own persons and become independent.

When these children grow up and leave their families, they look for another person they can depend on (co-dependence), to continue the process. It is a normal progression for people to go from one dependent relationship to another, including dependence on drugs and alcohol, when their parents prepare them from birth to stay dependent.

Independent Does Not Mean Alone

Many people have the mistaken idea that being an independent person means not needing anyone. They are afraid that if people in the family become independent they won't need parents or a partner and will leave the family. Some worry that if a family member is independent, it means doing whatever he or she likes with no regard for the rest of the family. Because of these beliefs, family members feel threatened when someone takes steps toward becoming independent. They may try to stop the process of growing toward independence and pull him or her back into a co-dependent relationship.

These fears are unfounded. Independence means people know what they think, what they feel, and what they want. It means they have skills to express what they think and feel to others in a respectful manner. It means they have skills to accomplish what they want most of the time, sometimes by themselves and sometimes with others. Only when family members become independent and express their uniqueness can they break the co-dependent patterns and move toward interdependence.

I Am Me, You Are You, and We Can Be Together

Interdependence is very different from co-dependence. Picture two people leaning on each other for support.

If one moves, the other falls. This is co-dependence. Now picture those same two people near each other and available to help and connect, but with lives of their own and skills of their own. There is a lot of give and take through respect and support for individual differences. This is interdependence.

Most people fantasize about interdependence when they think about building a relationship or a family. Then, without realizing it, they sabotage interdependence when their fears keep them holding on and refusing to let go.

Breaking the Cycle of Co-Dependence

Because parents in recovery have a lot of dependency issues, they need to learn a style of parenting that promotes independence and interdependence rather than co-dependence. Throughout this book, we stress such a style. In this chapter, we'd like to show how a family started to change their parenting style by giving up control.

These parents learned to maintain freedom with order; the parents don't control the children, nor do the children control the parents and the family. Instead, they learned to control their *own* behavior. They practiced emotional honesty (see Chapter 2) and shared what they thought and felt while encourging their kids to do the same. Instead of trying to "fix" everything, they made sure all the people involved in the problems were part of the solution. Finally, they said no where appropriate, without excuses or explanations.

The following case study shows how these skills were used to change co-dependent patterns in a family.

Sharon's Side of the Story

Sharon met Phil in an AA group while both were in early recovery. She had ended seven years, beginning when she was 15, of dependence of drugs. She still didn't feel like a whole person though, and started spending time with Phil with the expectation that he would fill the gap left when she gave up drugs. She went from one dependence to another by becoming dependent on Phil.

Sharon's dependency issues did not show up until Phil's daughter came to spend time with them. When Phil spent time with his 4-year-old daughter, Renae, Sharon felt threatened and jealous. She was afraid Phil wouldn't have any time or love left for her. She reacted by becoming distant and sullen. When Phil tried to include her in the time he spent with his daughter, Sharon met his attempts with anger and resistance. She used the excuse that Renae was a spoiled brat.

Phil's Side of the Story

Phil had neglected his daughter when he was using drugs. He remembers leaving his then infant daughter sleeping alone at home while he went out to get a six-pack of beer. After starting recovery, Phil allowed his guilt and shame to dictate his parenting. Now he overindulged Renae in an attempt to make up for past neglect. Because Phil only had weekends with his daughter, he thought he had to spend all his time with her, and he felt guilty if he spent exclusive time with Sharon. He wanted Sharon to spend every minute with Renae, too, to help him make up for past neglect. The more he overindulged, however, the more demanding Renae became. She *did* act like a spoiled brat sometimes.

It is amazing how many parents who do not have their children full time, feel they must put their entire life on hold and spend every available minute with the visiting children. It is more respectful to everyone when they maintain a semblance of their normal routine and each person has both time alone and time with the others.

The Co-Dependence Cycle

So both Sharon and Phil were co-dependent. Sharon was depending on Phil to make her whole, and Phil was trying to control Sharon by expecting her to treat his daughter the same way he did. That set up a co-dependence cycle.

Phil felt desperate enough to try anything. Finally, a friend in Phil's AA group told him about the parenting class he was attending.

Moving from Dependence to Independence to Interdependence

It didn't take Phil long to realize his behavior was not healthy for anyone involved. He decided to change his parenting style, using skills he learned in the parenting class. First he shared his thoughts and feelings by telling Sharon how he felt about the situation and what he wanted and why. He said,"I feel worried about your relationship with my daughter, and I'm afraid you won't like each other. I'm afraid that could lead to me thinking I have to choose between you, and I love you both. I want us to create a family together so no one is left out."

Then Phil controlled his behavior by deciding what *he* would do instead of what he wanted Sharon to do. He stopped pushing Sharon and Renae together and had faith in their ability to work out their relationship with each other. Instead of feeling guilty and trying to make it up to his daughter for his past mistakes, he found ways to express his feelings. He told Renae he loved her and wanted to spend time with her, and that he also wanted time alone and time with Sharon.

Phil and Renae sat down at the kitchen table with a calendar and scheduled special times for fun together. They made a list of things they enjoyed doing together. When the scheduled time arrived, they would look at the list and decide what they wanted to do together.

Phil learned to say no to his daughter's demands for constant attention and to suggest she spend time alone sometimes. He helped Renae make a list of things she enjoyed doing alone, like coloring, playing with her cars and village set, and playing with her giant Legos. When she became demanding, Phil would offer her a choice of two things from her list to do alone. At first, Renae would pout and say she didn't want to do either. Phil would say, "I'm sure you can find something to do. I'm busy right now." Then he would leave the room. When Renae realized her pouting was not effective, she stopped pouting and entertained herself.

Phil also told Renae she could stay with a sitter occasionally so he and Sharon could go out for coffee or take a walk. He explained, "I enjoy our special time together very much. It is also important for me to have special time with Sharon."

Phil encouraged Sharon to express her feelings and concerns and promised to listen without getting defensive or telling her how to fix things. Sharon let Phil know how angry she felt when he tried to control her relationship with his daughter. She told him she appreciated his backing off and giving her space to deal with it in her way. Phil listened nondefensively and validated her feelings by telling her he could understand.

They decided to work out a plan together to set aside time for the three of them as a family, time for the two of them as a couple, and individual time for each of them with the child.

Sharon appreciated being included in planning "special time" with Renae, during which the two of them could do something both enjoyed together. They soon developed a comfortable relationship with each other by spending time alone without Phil being around watching them.

Sharon also worked on "growing herself up" so she didn't act like another child clinging to Phil. She got involved in a group to support her recovery process and developed activities and friends of her own. The more interests she found outside the family, the more Sharon enriched her life and the lives of her family.

These noncontrolling but "take-charge" parenting skills helped Sharon and Phil break their cycle of co-dependence and encouraged independence and interdependence for all of them. They learned to give up the roles of controller, protector, or helpless victim and learned to be leaders. They controlled their own behavior instead of trying to control each other. They listened to their internal voices, shared their thoughts and feelings, and listened to each other without being defensive or trying to fix things for the other. They created structure and routines together that replaced their controlling methods. Phil learned to say no to his daughter when it was appropriate. These steps helped them create an atmosphere of freedom with order, where the parents weren't controlling the children, nor was the child controlling the parents.

Resistance to Change

It is important to know that children (and most adults) are not usually ecstatic about change—even when it is good for them. The baby bird does not know it is good for her to be pushed out of the nest. People who have learned to be dependent, either from being overprotected or overcontrolled, will resist becoming independent because they are not secure in that role in the beginning. We will repeat this theme many times, in the hope you will not be discouraged by resistance because you are reminded that it is normal.

Co-Dependence Takes Many Forms

In families where someone is abusing drugs or alcohol, the focus is either on the drug or on the person using the drug, but not on parenting. Parenting in such families is inconsistent, unpredictable, and often abusive. Individual family members feel isolated and lonely, and are unable to define boundaries and set respectful limits. Children can't trust their parents or themselves. Family roles become confused and rigid. Parents feel guilty, out of control, ashamed, inadequate, and incompetent.

Sharon and Phil learned that building a family is a process that takes time and that relationships blossom when they aren't forced. When parenting focuses on helping children develop independence and interdependence, there is room for everyone in a family, and no one needs to use competition and rivalry to find his or her own place.

Sharon and Phil are each learning to be independent while inviting Renae and each other to become independent at the same time. Using skills that encourage independence and interdependence, they now often find they are treating everyone around them better than they themselves were treated as children. This new style of parenting was not always easy for Phil and Sharon, and it did not happen overnight. However, they were so pleased with the results for themselves and Renae that they were willing to keep going back to their new skills whenever they made mistakes.

When parents use skills to lead and guide, they help their children learn to be responsible, caring, and capable people with useful life skills—the traits of independence and interdependence. When parents use punishment and control, children learn the skills of rebellion or unhealthy pleasing—the traits of dependence and co-dependence. As each family member is encouraged and valued for being him- or herself, the family begins a healing process to break the cycle of co-dependence.

Chapter
5

Establish Routines and Structure

The effects of substance abuse in a family are chaos and insecurity. Creating routines and structure is important to eliminate the chaos and establish trust and security.

In families where parents are actively dependent on chemicals, they're rarely able to maintain regular routines. The children are constantly wondering what will be happening, because each day is different. There is little or no consistency. The only thing the children can count on is that life will be inconsistent.

Children can adjust to this, but at what price? They don't develop a smooth rhythm to events in the day, and they lack a sense of calm expectancy. Life generally is disordered and disorganized. Sometimes it is chaotic and crazy, and leaves children feeling scared, confused, and insecure—as in Marla's home.

Some mornings, when Marla got up she'd hear her mother, Janice, moving about in the kitchen. Then she knew when she got downstairs she'd find the shades up, the kitchen bright, and her mother making beakfast for her and her younger brother Jeffrey. On other mornings, when Marla got up she couldn't hear any sounds in the house. Then Marla knew her mother was still in bed, hung over from the night before. She knew that when she got downstairs the shades would be down, the kitchen would be dark, and she would have to make breakfast. She'd also make her lunch, as well as Jeffrey's, and see to it that he got off to school. Marla never knew what the scene would be until the morning.

In another home, 10-year-old Harry, and his 7-year-old brother, Bob, were sitting on the living room floor playing cards. Their mother, Helen, was in the kitchen finishing the dinner dishes. They heard Stan's motorcycle roar into the driveway. They looked at each other and continued playing. The door swung open and their dad stomped in. Their mom yelled from the kitchen, "Where the hell have you been, Stan? We waited until seven to eat, but the boys were hungry. You'll have to heat something up if you want to eat."

Stan ignored her and yelled at the boys, "Why the hell aren't you in bed?"

Harry protested, "It's too early, it's only 7:45. We're not babies."

Dad howled, "Get to bed now!"

Both boys threw the cards down and stormed off, with Harry muttering, "It's not fair."

The previous two evenings when Stan had come home late, he had sat down and played with the boys, letting them stay up past 10 o'clock. Harry felt confused and upset. He never knew what to expect from his dad. When he asked his mother about it, she cautioned him not to say anything that might set his dad off: "You know how he can get." Harry got the message that he'd better not make any waves. He was never told that it was his dad's use of drugs that caused his inconsistent behavior. After a while, Harry wasn't even aware of the anxious feeling he got in the pit of his stomach as evening approached.

For such children, school often provides the only relief in terms of consistency and routine. They know that at school each day begins with certain activities that are followed with other activities. Spelling takes place at a certain time, as does recess and lunch. There is a flow to most days. There is a predictable order and routine. At least there's some place where children can learn to trust.

In recovery, parents have the opportunity to turn the inconsistencies of the addict into the actions of a healthy parent by establishing routines and following through with them. It's important to create routines that are predictable, consistent, and respectful to all. This helps rebuild trust because routines are something the kids can learn to count on. The routine becomes the "boss," rather than the parents or the children dictating what will happen. Children have an opportunity to learn to focus on the needs of the situation. This means doing what needs to be done because it needs to be done.

Marla's Mother Gets Help

Marla's mother, Janice, entered an inpatient treatment center for chemical dependency. When she came home, Janice knew she wanted to be a better parent but she wasn't sure how to begin. She decided to get more involved in the morning routine. But Janice was surprised to see that now things got worse instead of better. She spent a lot of time in the mornings coaxing, nagging, and yelling at Jeffrey, who dawdled in his room playing with his toys instead of getting ready for school. Marla, who had been so helpful *before* Janice started treatment, now would come downstairs and make her own breakfast after her mother had already prepared the family breakfast. Then, with a look of defiance, Marla would leave the dirty pans and dishes in the sink and slam the door on her way to school. Janice was angry and upset by the chaos and disrespect.

When Janice first came home from the treatment facility, she noticed a flyer from school lying on her desk, advertising a workshop on positive parenting. At the time, she tossed it aside, thinking she wasn't interested and had too many other things to do. But after several weeks of aggravation with the kids in the morning, Janice remembered the flyer from school. She pulled it out and looked at it again. This time she realized that help was available and she didn't have to figure this out all by herself. She decided to attend the workshop on positive parenting.

Janice was excited to learn so many new ideas. In the parenting workshop, the instructor talked about the importance of involving all people who are part of a problem to be part of the solution. As Janice listened she realized why the morning routine was getting worse instead of better. Without meaning to, in her effort to be a better mother, she had been insensitive to the kids and discounted them and their needs.

Establishing Morning Routines

The next afternoon when the children came home from school, and things were calm, Janice invited them to sit down and talk. She began by telling them how unhappy she was about the chaos and disrespect in the morning. They agreed that it didn't feel good to them either.

Janice told Jeffrey that she would like to get him an alarm clock because she knew he could handle being responsible for getting up in the morning. They made a date to go to the store the next afternoon so he could pick out a clock. Janice told him he could spend up to $8. She promised to teach him how to use it when they got home.

Next she asked, "What are the things you need to do to be ready for school each day?" She was a little surprised to hear that he knew what he needed to do. Janice asked him if he needed help to get all this done. Jeffrey thought that Marla reminding him was a good idea. His mother began to realize how dependent Jeffrey was on his older sister.

She asked Marla what she needed to do each morning to be ready for school. She was surprised to find that Marla thought making breakfast was her responsibility. Janice exclaimed, "You both have a lot to do in the morning!" and asked Jeffrey if he'd like to make a chart to help him remember. The idea intrigued him, and Janice asked Marla if she'd be willing to help Jeffrey with his chart. (Janice wanted to help Marla feel included, but at the same time she was showing her that she didn't have to do everything.) Marla agreed to help Jeffrey make a chart that afternoon.

After the chart was completed, Janice helped them role-play what morning would look like when they followed their plan. Everyone laughed and had a good time. It was clear everyone knew what to do.

Realizing that making breakfast was important to Marla, Janice asked if they could work on a plan together. During their planning session, Janice realized how pressured her daughter was in the morning. She wanted to set up a routine where Marla could contribute without so much pressure. They decided Janice would make breakfast on school days and Marla would make breakfast for the family on Saturdays and Sundays.

Two days later, they were ready to implement the morning routine. Jeffery's alarm went off, and Janice noticed he was still in bed. She took a deep breath, resisted her temptation to wake him, and headed for the kitchen to begin breakfast. When she heard Marla coaxing her brother, Janice motioned to Marla and asked if she'd be willing to help her brother in a new way. "Would you being willing to help Jeffrey by giving him the opportunity to learn that he can handle getting himself up?"

Marla agreed and went back to getting ready for school. Janice went back to making breakfast. Janice soon heard Jeffrey scurrying around. He came into the kitchen just as it was time to leave and Marla was heading out the door. He said he was hungry, and Mother said, "I'll bet you are. Check your chart to see what happens now." When Jeffrey looked at his chart, he realized that it was time to leave for school. He dashed out the door feeling hungry. It only took a few days before Janice noticed that each child was getting up and ready without a fuss and Jeffrey seldom missed breakfast.

Jeffrey did not resist as much as some kids might. Janice had a plan ready to use if he had resisted. She would contact Jeffery's teacher and ask for her help. She would explain her plan for helping Jeffrey learn to be responsible for getting himself up and off to school in the mornings. She would ask the teacher if he would be willing to allow Jeffrey to experience the consequences of being late to school. He might stay in at recess or after school to make up the work he missed.

Janice was delighted with the results in her family when she set up routines. She had experienced success by following the guidelines for setting up routines that had been presented in her parenting workshop:

Six Guidelines for Setting Up Routines

1. Focus on one problem at a time.
2. When everyone is calm (not at the time of conflict), discuss the problem with the children.
3. Involve children in developing a routine. Ask for their ideas. When their ideas are not appropriate, use limited choices. For example, if your child says, "I don't want to do it at all," give a limited choice such as "You may do it before breakfast or before dinner. Not doing it at all isn't one of the choices."
4. Use visuals (charts, lists, timers).
5. Practice through role-playing.
6. Follow through with action in a firm and kind manner. (Refer to the chart or list, or ask, "What was our agreement?" Allow child to experience natural or logical consequences, but not punishment. Resist rescuing and lecturing.)

Establishing routines helps parents develop long-range benefits in their families. The long-range benefits are security, a calmer atmosphere, trust, and life skills for children. Children learn to be responsible for their own behavior, to feel capable, and to cooperate in the family.

Chemically dependent people are often looking for short-term results: the "quick fix." The quick fix may stop the problem temporarily. Nagging, prodding, and yelling may get the task done, but the long-range benefits are sacrificed.

When parents change their thinking and make a commitment to work for the long-range benefits, it's helpful to have steps to follow, such as the six guidelines for setting up routines. Also, it is helpful to be realistic and to understand that things may not work perfectly at first. Children who are used to behaving in certain ways need time before they believe their parents mean what they say. Remember, it is human nature to resist change, even when we want it or know it is good for us. When we understand this, we can keep following the plan until the resistance ends.

Janice was able to use what she had learned to help her friend Helen make some big changes in her family. Helen's husband, Stan, was an addict. Helen denied that he was an addict until her friend Janice confronted her and said, "You can't continue like this. Stan is out of control. I think he's an addict. I know the signs— I was one."

Helen buried her head in her hands and began to sob. Janice said, "You need help. I want you to go to a CODA (Co-Dependents Anonymous) meeting with me tomorrow." Helen began to attend meetings. The first thing Helen decided to focus on was the family's chaotic pattern at bedtime. She asked Stan if he would like to help make bedtime more pleasant and secure for the kids. He said, "Leave me alone. I'm not interested in your psychology stuff."

Helen was upset, but she learned to focus on herself and look to see what changes *she* could make, instead of trying to change Stan.

Establishing Bedtime Routines

Janice had told Helen about the guidelines for setting up routines. On Saturday she sat down with her two sons, 10-year-old Harry and 7-year-old Bob, and asked them how they felt about what happened at bedtime. Bob started to cry, and Harry said he hated being yelled at. Helen agreed that bedtime was hard on everyone, and that she wanted to make it better and needed their help.

They talked about what would be a reasonable bedtime. Harry was older, and he wanted to stay up later than his brother. Helen gave each of the boys a limited choice: Bob could pick either 7:45 or 8, and Harry could choose either 8:15 or 8:30. On Fridays and Saturdays, both boys could stay up until 9 if they wanted. Bob picked 8 and Harry decided on 8:30. Next she asked them what they had to do to get ready for bed. Each boy came up with a list (pajamas on, teeth brushed, floor picked up, bathroom cleaned). Helen suggested they each make a chart and post it on the door to their room. She also helped them figure out how much time it would take to do each thing. Bob decided he needed thirty minutes, and Harry decided he needed fifteen minutes.

Helen asked if the boys would like time for a bedtime story. Both thought that was a great idea. Helen told them she would be available for fifteen minutes before lights-out time for each of them. They decided that she'd read to Bob and listen to Harry read to her. They added up the time they needed to get everthing done and, working backward, set the time to start getting ready. For Bob it was 7:15, and for Harry it was 8.

Both boys got busy making their chart. Bob pasted pictures of all the things he had to do. Harry used markers to print his chart and added stickers to it. They posted the charts and role-played their plan. At the beginning of the role play, it became clear that Bob didn't know when it was time to start. Helen suggested she could announce the time and set the timer. Bob agreed, and they practiced again.

Helen told the boys she would talk to their dad and let him know what they were doing. She also told them that the reason their dad behaved the way he did was because he was taking drugs—it wasn't anything *they* were doing. (See Chapter 8 for more information on talking to kids about drugs.)

The next night both boys were playing in the living room. Helen said, "It's 7:15," and set the timer. She went into the kitchen to finish the dishes. At 7:45 she was sitting on Bob's bed waiting while he was finishing in the bathroom. He hurried into his pj's, and at 7:55 Helen began reading. At 8 she stopped reading and turned out the light. Bob cried, "No fair, you didn't finish the story." Helen didn't respond. She bent down and kissed him and walked out of the room. Bob continued to complain, but Helen didn't say anything. After awhile he was quiet.

Harry had been watching TV with his dad. When he got up to start getting ready, Stan said, "Why don't you stay here with me?" Helen came in and asked to talk to Stan in the other room. "Stan, the boys and I have worked out a plan for bedtime, and I need your help to make it work." He asked, "Does it matter if he stays up a little later?" She replied, "We have a plan, and I need your help." He shrugged and went back to watching TV.

Harry got busy getting ready, and at 8:15 Helen came into his room and asked what he wanted to read. Harry read from his favorite book. At 8:30 Helen said, "It's lights-out time," and kissed him goodnight. She followed through with the plan each night, and the family became comfortable with the routine. With few exceptions, bedtimes were calmer. Eventually Stan recognized how well the bedtime routine was working, and when he was home and sober he also got involved with the story time.

Helen had learned that she didn't have to wait for Stan to change; she could change on her own. She felt much better about herself when she decided what she would do to change and followed a plan that helped her accomplish her goals.

Parents have many opportunities to set up routines with their children. The more families establish routines, the more they experience organization, structure, and order. For example, mealtime is another area where chaos is often the norm until routines are established.

Establishing Dinner Time Routines

Providing a sense of order at dinner time can set a positive tone for the rest of the evening. Here is a typical scene in the Wilson family *before* they learned a dinner routine:

Zach had just arrived home after picking up his two children at the baby-sitter's. It was 7:30 already! The children were complaining they were hungry. Ruff, the family dog, was jumping on everyone, looking for food. Zach hadn't remembered to thaw anything for dinner. His wife, Amy, had been gone only three days, and he was "losing it." She was in a treatment center to get help with her dependence on prescription drugs. Zach knew he couldn't continue like this much longer.

With the help of the family counselor at the treatment facility, Zach decided that a routine at dinner time would eliminate the chaos and help create order. His children, Liz (5) and Greg (9), wanted to help. They sat down together Sunday after breakfast to plan what they could do. First they talked about the different jobs that needed to be done. The list included setting the table, cooking dinner, and washing the dishes. Zach reminded them of Ruff. "Oh yeah, let's add feeding Ruff to the list," they said.

After looking at the list, Liz said she wanted to set the table and Greg said he wanted to feed Ruff. Zach said for this week he'd make dinner and wash the dishes. He also decided to make arrangements at work to leave earlier, so he could pick up the children by 5:30.

After just one day of the new plan, he noticed how much calmer things seemed. The next week they met and decided this was working so well they'd continue. Liz said next week she wanted to feed the dog. Zach suggested that at their next meeting they talk about rotating jobs. Next Sunday, they decided Liz would feed the dog, and Greg would set the table and make macaroni and cheese on Tuesday night. Liz then said she wanted to make dinner one night, too. Zach asked her what she wanted to make. After thinking for a minute she said, "My favorite, hot dogs." Zach was delighted and said that after their meeting he'd teach her how to use the microwave.

The next week they made some more changes and finally settled on the kids each week alternating the jobs of feeding the dog and setting the table. The kids each decided to make dinner one night a week and do the dishes together one night. Zach said he'd take the family out to dinner one night and suggested they use paper plates two nights. Everyone was looking forward to Amy coming home and participating with them in their new routines.

After three weeks in treatment, Amy came home. She felt uncertain and overwhelmed by the changes Zach and the kids had made. She thought, "It's my job to cook. Maybe they don't really need me." And she told the kids that they didn't have to cook or do dishes anymore. She was home now and would take over. The kids protested, "We *like* to help!" Amy insisted, "It's *my* job!"

Zach felt angry. The new routine was working. He enjoyed cooperating and wanted to continue. He also knew the kids were feeling good about the skills they were learning. Zach suspected that when Amy went back to work the following week and added meetings to her schedule that life would become hectic again. He hoped she would realize that their new mealtime routine benefited the entire family.

By the end of her first week back to work, Amy was frazzled. Picking up the kids at the sitter's, stopping at the store to buy groceries, cooking dinner, cleaning up, and dashing out to her meetings was taking its toll. Zach said he'd be happy to get the kids, or do the shopping, or make dinner; but Amy insisted that she could handle it all.

By the end of the second week, Zach was really scared. He thought Amy was heading for a relapse. She was moody and irritable, jumping on everyone. It was a relief when she left for her meeting each evening.

When she returned from her meeting, Zach was waiting. He told her how frightened he was and that it wasn't working to have her trying to do everything. She seemed angry and irritable most of the time. He was tired of her getting angry with the kids. He was sure they could all work together. The routine they had set up when she was in treatment had worked so well they could continue with it now.

Amy was shocked and defensive. She said, "How dare you criticize me after all I've been through! I suppose you think you're a better parent than I am!" She got up and went to bed. The next morning she told Zach that he could pick the kids up at the sitter's—she'd be going to her meeting straight from work. Because he was obviously more competent than she was, he could do it all. He told her he was sorry that she saw it that way and said he hoped that someday soon she would be willing to work together with the rest of the family.

Zach explained to the children what had happened, and they decided to resume their mealtime routine. After that, Amy rarely ate with the family.

Not every situation has a "happy ending." It can be very difficult for some families when not all members want to participate (often they join in later), but it certainly is possible to set up routines with the willing members and it's worth it.

The guidelines for setting up routines can be used to set up time for yourself, time for couples to spend together, times for families to interact and have fun, quality time for parents to focus on one child at a time, homework time, and time for family members to work together doing jobs such as cleaning the bathrooms, vacuuming, and dusting.[1]

Establishing routines is a method whereby family members learn to cooperate, to connect, and to feel capable. It also fosters the re-establishment of trust by replacing chaos with routine and structure.

---

[1]For more information on establishing routines and getting the whole family involved in a smooth-running household, we recommend *Family Work: Whose Job Is It?* by Lynn Lott, Riki Intner, and Marilyn Kientz (Petaluma, CA: Practical Press, 1988).

Chapter
6

Set Limits and Follow Through

Picture yourself standing on a cliff. You walk to the edge and lean over. There's a deep drop. Your foot hits a stone that tumbles over the edge and bounces down the steep sides to the chasm below. What do you feel as you stand there watching? Do you feel a knot of fear in your stomach?

Now picture yourself on the same cliff, but this time as you approach the edge you find a thick steel railing firmly embedded in the ground. You feel how solid it is. As you look over the edge, what do you feel this time? A little uneasy perhaps, but calmer and more secure while hanging on to the railing?

Everyone feels more secure and comfortable with limits. Limits provide a foundation of safety and security in the family. When chemical dependency is present in families, there are usually threats of limits, but no one follows through on the threats. The safety and security of real limits are missing. Members of the family often feel that knot of fear, insecurity, and frustration in their stomachs. The negative feelings are often covered and hidden by negative behavior: demands, anger, depression, drinking, fighting, violence. The Browns provide an example of what happens when limits and follow-through are absent.

Every Sunday the Browns take their two boys, 6-year-old Gordy and 9-year-old Johnny, to McDonald's. By the time they leave, Dad has already had a six-pack of beer, so Mom decides to drive. The scene never varies. A few blocks from home, the kids start fighting in the back seat. Mom, angry about Dad's drinking, hardly hears them as she broods and drives. Dad, however, threatens the boys. "If you guys don't stop fighting, we're going home! I mean it!"

The boys have heard this many times and know Dad doesn't follow through on his threats, so they get louder and louder as they continue to fight. Mom finally gets into the act, yelling and trying to hit them while she drives the car. When she starts counting to three, the boys quiet down until they arrive at the restaurant. They wait until the food is ordered and then start fighting again.

Mom tries to ignore them and hopes Dad will do the same. She wants to avoid the scene and embarrassment that follows when Dad, with a six-pack under his belt, starts hitting the boys in the restaurant. The boys escalate the fight until Dad, swearing and screaming, grabs them, spanks them, and sends them to the car without any dinner.

Similar scenes occur in many families on a regular basis when parents seem unable to set firm and clear limits. Instead, they resort to coaxing, nagging, yelling, threatening, and hitting. But these parenting techniques do not work, and they damage the relationship between parent and child. Children learn not to pay attention to adults who nag and yell. The lack of respect is felt by all. The children continue to push limits and test adults until, as in the Brown family, the situation escalates to violence. Everyone in the family ends up feeling badly.

An important part of clean and sober parenting is learning to establish boundaries and to set limits. Boundaries and limits are meaningless without follow-through. If you say it, mean it; and if you mean it, follow through with dignity and respect.

Mr. Brown stopped drinking and began attending AA meetings. As time passed and he progressed in his recovery, he decided he wanted to take an active role in parenting his sons. At the same time, Mrs. Brown attended Al-Anon meetings and learned to focus more on herself than on her husband. She began to become clearer about what she wanted for herself and realized how important it was for her family to believe she meant what she said. They both decided they wanted to treat their children more respectfully. Then they attended a parenting workshop where they learned the four steps to limit setting.

Four Steps to Limit Setting

There are four steps to limit setting: think it through, identify your limits, communicate your limits, and follow through.

Step 1. Think It Through

The first step is to think about who "owns" the problem. Is the problem your child's business, yours, or something that concerns both parent and child? Too often parents perpetuate co-dependency by dealing with problems that children can handle themselves and learn from their mistakes. Examples of this include allowing children to experience the consequences of not wearing a jacket on a cold day, wearing mismatched clothing, or reading late into the night in their room and being tired the next day. If the problem you are concerned about belongs to your child, letting go is a more appropriate skill to practice. If the problem is yours, go to the next step.

Step 2. Identify Your Limits

The second step is to clearly identify your limits. It is important, as a recovering parent, to discover what you want and what you will or won't tolerate. A healthy part of personal growth is to know you have a right to limits and to acknowledge to yourself and others what they are. For some people, recognizing their right to have limits is a major step in developing a sense of self-respect. When you have self-respect, it is easier to show respect to others when you communicate your limits.

Step 3. Communicate Your Limits

Once you identify your limits, you need to let others know what they are. An effective and respectful method for communicating your limits to children is through offering limited choices. This allows freedom of choice within safe boundaries, and usually prevents power struggles. Choose two alternatives you can live with, and let your children choose which is best for them. It is helpful to ask children for their ideas for solutions to the problem. If they can come up with an option you can live with, they will feel respected if you choose their alternative. If they suggest an alternative you cannot live with, show respect for yourself by saying, "That's not a choice that works for me. You'll need to choose one of the first two choices until we can come up with a different solution. Which one works best for you?" Like most people, children enjoy having options and are interested in cooperating when they have a choice.

Step 4. Follow Through

Once you've communicated your limits, follow through with action. Do what you said you'd do, in a firm, kind manner. Because following through is a new concept for recovering families, you can expect your children to test your ability to do what you've said you'll do. Based on their past experience, they won't believe the words at first. This is all the more reason to follow through. Don't become discouraged by the testing and disbelief. Know it is normal and continue to follow through with dignity and respect.

Limit Setting in Real Life

Let's go back to the Brown family and see how setting limits helped in their recovery process and created more security in their family. Because Mr. Brown had decided to take a more active role in parenting, he sat down and talked with Mrs. Brown about their unpleasant trips to McDonald's. They talked about who owned the problem, as recommended in Step 1 of the follow-through process. They both agreed that the problem was theirs, because they didn't enjoy being out in public with fighting boys. The safety of the family was also at stake when the boys fought in the car.

The parents then followed Step 2 and defined their limits. Mr. Brown thought it was reasonable to want to eat in a restaurant without having to put up with fighting boys. They both were clear that they were unwilling to drive the car if the boys were fighting, as it was not safe.

The Browns decided to follow Step 3 and communicate their limits to Johnny and Gordy. The next evening, right after dinner, the family sat down together to talk about restaurant and car manners. Mrs. Brown began by describing the problem as she saw it. Mr. Brown agreed and added that by the end of such evenings he was feeling angry and wanted things to be more pleasant for everyone. The boys just giggled and punched each other.

Mrs. Brown asked the boys if they had any ideas of how to improve the car or restaurant scenes. Neither had any ideas, so Mrs. Brown shared her idea. "It's not safe to drive the car with you two fighting in the back seat. If you choose to fight, I'll pull over and wait for you to stop. I'm willing to drive only if I feel it's safe for all of us." Mr. Brown told the boys he'd do the same thing when he was driving.

Mr. Brown said, "On Sunday, we'll ask if you would like to go to McDonald's with us. If you do, we'll go, but if you start fighting in the restaurant, we'll go back home and try again the next Sunday. Mom and I don't enjoy eating out with all the chaos."

Both boys said, "Fine."

The Testing Phase

It's wonderful when things work exactly as planned but they seldom do. When children are confronted with a new pattern of behavior, they often test to see what their parents will do. They are used to adults who use words to threaten, but who seldom follow through with actions until they are angry and unreasonable. Children are willing players in the game and provoke adults to anger by not responding until the adults are angry.

It can take time to break old habits and patterns, even with consistent follow-through. Even though Gordy and Johnny had agreed to the new routine, they tested their parents. But Mr. and Mrs. Brown were ready with their plan to follow through.

Follow-Through

On Sunday, Mr. Brown asked the boys if they would like to go to McDonald's. They both said yes and made a beeline for the car. When the boys started fighting a few blocks from home, instead of the nagging that used to take place Mr. and Mrs. Brown looked at each other and squeezed each other's hand to offer support. Mrs. Brown pulled the car over to wait for the fighting to stop. A few minutes later, the boys stopped fighting and the Browns continued to drive to McDonald's.

Before the Browns had even finished ordering the food, the boys began fighting again. Mr. and Mrs. Brown looked at each other, winked, and told the clerk to cancel their order. When the boys realized what was happening, they promised to stop the fight. Mrs. Brown smiled and said, "We'll try again next Sunday."

Gordy continued his protests and pleaded to stay at McDonald's. Mr. and Mrs. Brown turned toward the door and walked out of the restaurant and into the car. They waited a few minutes until the boys joined them. Gordy was very angry and cursed his parents under his breath. Johnny sat in the back seat crying softly. Mrs. Brown drove home in silence, got out of the car, and both parents went in the kitchen to begin making dinner. Johnny, noticing what was happening, began to set the table, all the while mumbling under his breath that it wasn't fair.

When parents give children the opportunity to try again, they are being respectful to themselves and to the child. They are saying, "I am going to maintain routine and follow through." They are also saying to the child, "It is OK if you make a mistake. Anyone can make a mistake. You have an opportunity to try again."

The following week, the boys were quiet in the car, but once the food was ordered they started chasing each other through the restaurant, yelling and threatening to hit each other. Mr. and Mrs. Brown waited for the food, and then walked quietly to the car. Johnny and Gordy came out of the restaurant crying. Both boys were talking at the same time trying to blame the other for starting the fight. When Mrs. Brown started the engine, Johnny shouted, "You don't care about me!" Mrs. Brown gently took Johnny's hand and led him to the back seat of the car without saying a word. Johnny put on his seat belt, crying, "Nobody cares about me."

Once the family arrived back home, things were quiet. The boys were getting the picture and realized their complaints did not change anything. The food was put on the table, and everyone ate in silence. Mr. and Mrs. Brown felt less exhausted than on previous outings. Even though the kids hassled them, they had a goal and a plan to reach that goal. They congratulated each other on what felt like clear progress.

Next week, the family enjoyed a trip to McDonald's without any hassles. Occasionally, in the weeks that followed, Mr. or Mrs. Brown would pull the car over if the boys were fighting, but soon even that stopped. With hard work, time, and courage, Mr. and Mrs. Brown followed through with their plan.

Five Traps That Defeat Effective Follow-Through

Because follow-through is such an important part of limit setting, it is easier to learn if you are aware of the traps that defeat effective follow-through.

1. Not Getting Specific Agreements in Advance

Not having agreements (that include a specific time) creates power struggles and makes follow-through more difficult. Agreements make it easier to get through the resistance phase because kids know it is reasonable for parents to expect them to keep "their" agreements. Mr. and Mrs. Brown talked to the boys about the changes they wanted to make and invited their participation in the planning.

2. Expecting Children to Have the Same Priorities as Adults

Parents forget that children have different priorities from adults. They usually agree to things that are important to adults, such as going to bed at a reasonable time and doing chores, but that doesn't mean it is important to them, as it is to adults. Actually, they don't care about going to bed at a reasonable time and doing chores. They have different priorities and concerns appropriate to their age. Parents can save their sanity when they accept this difference and expect their children to act age-appropriately. Acting age-appropriately means the children are normal when they forget to do the things they have agreed to do just to please adults. Expect them to forget. Don't get upset, just follow through.

3. Lack of Understanding for Different Styles

It's imortant to understand and allow for different "styles" of reaction to change. Some children go along with the changes adults want to make. Others resist and test. They may stomp and yell or throw tantrums to get their parents to back down. It is like putting quarters in a soda machine when nothing comes out. Some people walk away, while others shake or kick the machine. Others bang and pound and yell at it, redoubling their efforts to get a "response."

It's important not to be sidetracked by your children's responses to change and to remain focused on the goal to follow through on what you say you'll do. Focus reserves your energy and increases chances for success. Mr. Brown allowed Johnny to be angry and was not manipulated when he yelled, "No one cares about me." It's all right for children to be angry when faced with constructive changes in the family. Their anger will not last when they consistently experience positive results.

4. Failing to Stick to the Plan

Too many parents *say* what they'll do, but when it comes time to *do* it, they revert to patterns of reminding, nagging, threatening, and punishing. Rudolf Dreikurs, a psychiatrist who worked closely with Alfred Adler, emphasized the importance of acting rather than talking.[1] We know this is difficult for most parents. Having a plan helps. If Mrs. Brown had reminded the boys that she was going to pull the car over, she would be back into her old patterns of reminding and nagging.

---

[1]See Rudolf Dreikurs, *Children: The Challenge* (New York: Hawthorn, 1964).

5. Not Maintaining Dignity and Respect for Child and Adult

It is essential to follow through in a firm, kind manner. Had either Mr. or Mrs. Brown squeezed their sons' hands in anger while following through, or yelled at them, or insulted them, they would have been being disrespectful. When parents don't maintain an attitude of dignity and respect, they invite children to stop focusing on their behavior and to focus instead on shame or the unfairness of their parents.

Setting Limits with Follow-Through Works

In the previous situation, both Mr. and Mrs. Brown had made a commitment to make changes in their parenting styles. Even though the kids felt good to be included in a new plan to make things better, they tested the change. Mr. and Mrs. Brown expected their resistance as normal, and were ready with a plan to follow through. Following through, with dignity and respect, is the key to a relatively smooth transition through the resistance phase. Without follow-through, it is too easy to get discouraged by the resistance, assume that the plan for change isn't working, and revert to nagging, yelling, and violence.

Consistency Is Nice, but . . .

Consistency between parents is nice, but it is not always present. In this case, Mr. and Mrs. Brown worked together. In some families, only one parent is committed to change.

This can work fine, because children respond differently to the behavior of different adults. They will respond one way to the parent who sets limits and follows through, and another way to the parent who doesn't. You can decide what you will to do to follow through with dignity and respect even if your spouse chooses a different style.

Another Family Benefits from Follow-Through

Peter lived with his small son, Scott. Before going into treatment, Peter was smoking marijuana daily. He would get home from work, light a joint, and fix dinner. The trouble started when he called Scott to come eat.

Peter wanted to eat at the table. Scott wanted to eat dinner in front of the television set. Peter did not know how to work out an agreement with Scott and follow through. Instead, Scott would badger him to eat in the living room. Peter would give in, light another joint, read the newspaper while he ate, and enjoy being left to himself.

Scott learned that when he wanted something he could manipulate until his father gave in. And Peter learned he could escape into his own world after giving in to Scott's demands, and thus avoid dealing with the hassles.

Once he was in recovery, Peter saw Scott as a spoiled, demanding child who was unpleasant to be around. He knew he had contributed to Scott's behavior by being so lax as a parent, but he wasn't sure how to change. When he decided to get help, he chose a therapist with expertise in parenting education.

The therapist asked Peter to give an example of a typical problem. Peter shared, "Every time we go to the store, Scott demands money to buy something. I guess that's because manipulation has worked so well in the past, Scott continues his demands until I give in. I feel angry at myself for giving in, and guilty for not liking to be around my own son."

The therapist suggested that shopping would be a good area in which to practice setting limits and following through. Peter and his therapist talked about setting up a plan with limits, the testing Peter could expect from Scott, and then role-played how Peter could follow through effectively.

Peter set up an allowance for Scott, who thought the idea of having his own money was great. They negotiated an amount they both thought was reasonable and set up a payday. They agreed that Scott could spend his money as he wished, but that Peter wouldn't give him any extra money or make any loans to him in between paydays.

Scott received his money and on their first trip to the store spent his entire allowance for a toy he "had to have." Peter curbed his temptation to comment. The next day Scott found something else he wanted at the store. Peter asked, "Do you have your money?" Scott said, "I spent it yesterday. You give me the money." Peter replied, "Payday is Friday." Scott continued his demands. Peter ignored Scott's demands and finished his shopping.

Peter was amazed at how closely Scott followed the predictions of the therapist. He was glad the role-playing had prepared him. Otherwise he would not have been able to control his anger when Scott became so demanding at the store. He still found it difficult to remain firm and kind when he felt like saying mean things to Scott. There were times when he was tempted to give in to his son just to get some peace. His parenting education helped—he realized he'd be settling for a short-term solution while perpetuating a long-term problem.

Next they tackled the dinner problem. They agreed that they would take turns, eating in front of the TV and at the table every other day. On the days they were supposed to eat in front of the TV, they would push the mute button during commercials so they could talk about the program they were watching.

On the days they had agreed to sit at the table, Scott often objected at first. Peter would turn the TV off, take Scott by the hand, and walk to the table with him. Scott fell on the floor and had a temper tantrum the first time his dad followed through this way. Peter sat at the table and waited quietly for Scott to stop screaming. Then he said, "What was our agreement?" Scott pouted. Peter said, "I can hardly wait for you to remember our agreement. I really miss you at the table." Scott continued to pout. Peter continued to eat, but didn't say any more.

When Peter finished eating, he left the table and said, "I'll be back to help you clean up in ten minutes." Ten minutes later, Scott was still pouting and hadn't eaten anything. Peter cleaned up the kitchen without saying anything. (They hadn't worked on an agreement about cleaning up yet.)

Later that evening, Scott went into the kitchen and made himself a peanut butter sandwich. Peter did not say anything, even when Scott left a mess. He knew how important it was to work on one thing at a time, and he did not want to participate in a power struggle.

The next night they had a pleasant time watching TV and talking while they ate. And the *next* night, when Peter called Scott to the dinner table Scott turned off the TV and came to dinner. He had learned that his manipulation tactics did not work, and he really wanted to be with his dad.

Kids feel better about themselves when they keep their agreements and are not allowed to manipulate. However, they don't know this until they have time to experience it. Scott learned that his father meant what he said because Peter learned to follow through. They both enjoyed the security and good feelings of their improved relationship.

Inappropriate Follow-Through

Sometimes parents use the concept of follow-through inappropriately and then wonder why it is ineffective. Sylvia, a single parent, lived with her 12-year-old daughter, Monica, and her 15-year-old son Michael. Monica had been experiencing difficulty with her school work for several years. Sylvia knew Monica was capable of doing the work. She thought Monica was just being lazy and irresponsible when she didn't do her homework or forgot to bring it to school. Her teachers had called Sylvia and told her about the situation.

Sylvia believed that as a parent it was her business to get Monica to do her homework. When reminding and nagging didn't work, she grounded Monica and told her she wasn't allowed to meet her friends after school. Monica was ordered to come straight home and do her homework. Sylvia hoped she could make Monica feel bad enough to realize she had to get her homework done.

But Monica's teachers reported that her homework still wasn't getting done. So Sylvia took away TV and telephone privileges and told Monica she had to sit at the table every evening until she completed her assignments.

Then Sylvia went to school and met with Monica's teachers. She took their advice to remind her daughter each night that she had homework to do. But Monica still didn't respond to this by doing her homework. Sylvia was so frustrated that she finally gave up. She sat on the couch and cried. It was at this point that she remembered similar scenes from her childhood.

Sylvia had grown up in a family where most nights her father drank. He would stand over her and pound on the table as she struggled with her homework. He yelled at her, berated her, and grounded her. Sylvia would cry and feel bad, but did not improve in getting her homework done. Although she had promised herself at the time she would never be like her father, she now saw how often she acted just like him with her daughter.

Sylvia mistakenly believed that as long as she was "doing something" she was following through. In fact, she was actually being co-dependent by "doing for" her daughter and taking on a problem that belonged to Monica. Meeting with the teachers without Monica and continually reminding and nagging removed Monica from responsibility for her problem. When that didn't work, Sylvia switched her co-dependent behavior by "doing to" her daughter with threats and punishment. Grounding, taking away privileges, and coercion are not respectful ways of dealing with problem situations. "Doing for" or "doing to" is not appropriate follow-through.

Doing "with" Instead of Doing "for" or Doing "to"

Sylvia found a parent education center that offered a drop-in parent support group. She learned that "doing *with*" her daughter was a way of developing effective follow-through strategies. Sylvia was excited to tackle the long-standing problem of homework. She shared the problem with the group, and the group members helped her develop a plan to turn the problem over to Monica.

Sylvia let Monica know that from now on she would be available to help her, if asked, but that she would not remind or nag her anymore. She said to Monica,

"I have faith in you that you can handle this problem, and learn whatever you need to learn from your choices."

In this case, Sylvia's job to follow through meant doing less rather than more. Turning the problem over to Monica, letting go, and not trying to control her daughter's behavior was difficult for Sylvia. It was especially hard for her when the teachers called, but she told them, "I appreciate your concern. I'll put Monica on the phone so you can work it out with her."

It was also difficult to watch Monica make poor choices and experience failure while she was learning that she was responsible for the consequences of her choices. With the support and encouragement of the group, Sylvia was able to stay out of Monica's homework problem. It took time, but gradually Sylvia was able to see improvement and experience a friendlier relationship with her daughter.

Walking the Talk

Many parents in recovery do a great job of talking, but find it difficult to "walk the talk"—to do, as well as to say. Follow-through is an opportunity to practice walking the talk. Just saying something to kids isn't going to make change happen. Good intentions and well-executed planning sessions fall flat when parents don't follow through with kind, firm action.

Setting limits and following through is an extremely effective method for positive results for both parents and children. It provides children with the limits they need to feel safe and secure while learning responsibility. And it provides parents with a plan to create order instead of chaos.

▼

Chapter

7

Learn Healthy Communication Skills

People get better at whatever they practice. When you practice unhealthy communication skills, you get better at unhealthy communication. When you practice healthy communication skills, you get better at healthy communication.

Chemically dependent, co-dependent households practice unhealthy rules of communication: "Don't feel, don't talk, and don't trust." That style of communication is restrictive and isolating. Recovering families have the opportunity to begin practicing a completely different style of communication. This new style is open and invites healing. The information in this chapter shows how to move from unhealthy communication to healthy communication.

Communication means simply that one person sends a message to another person, who receives it and then gives a reaction to the person who sent the original message. Communication can be either with words or with actions—it can be verbal or nonverbal. It can also be vertical or horizontal. The first key to healthy communication is understanding the difference between vertical and horizontal communication.

Vertical and Horizontal Communication

When we communicate vertically, we make comparisons of right or wrong and good or bad. The focus is on one-up-manship. Rudolph Dreikurs called this kind of communication "deflating to inflate." Someone ends up in a deflated (inferior) position so someone else can feel inflated (superior). When you gain a sense of superiority at the expense of someone else, you may feel temporarily secure; however, to maintain that superior positon you pay a heavy price—you have to keep others down. When you do this, you discourage others, provoke feelings of inadequacy and insecurity, reinforce inequality, blame, judge, criticize, and dwell on rightness or wrongness. Vertical communication diminishes everyone's self-confidence and self-esteem.

When you learn to communicate horizontally, however, you recognize your own basic worth and the worth of others. When your communication is horizontal, you stress cooperation instead of power over others. You look for solutions instead of blame. You value differences and encourage uniqueness. Horizontal communication stresses mutual respect, in which you value yourself and value others. You don't take responsibility for anyone's behavior but your own. You know that the only person you can change is yourself. Self-confidence and self-esteem increases for everyone through horizontal communication.

The following quiz lets you know if your communication is horizontal or vertical. The more "yes" answers you have, the more horizontal your communication.

1. Does your communication treat others as equals?
2. Does your communication encourage others to be themselves and know they are unconditionally accepted for who they are?
3. Does your communication invite disclosure and discussion that focuses on how you can help each other?
4. Does your communication value differences and explore alternatives that respect the values of all concerned through problem solving and give and take?
5. Does your communication search for an understanding of what others mean by being curious and asking questions that invite clarification and deeper meaning?
6. Is your communication such that you feel free to express what you think, feel, and want without expecting others to think the same, feel the same, or give you what you want?

A Recovering Family Practices Respectful Communication

Julie and Ed each had chemically dependent fathers. Ed had followed his father's path and had used marijuana daily since he was 13. Julie had followed her mother's path and had engaged in co-dependent behaviors with Ed. They had both been in recovery for one year.

Julie and Ed loved their three daughters, but they didn't have any positive parenting skills. They didn't like the fact that they were repeating the unhealthy patterns they grew up with, so they decided to take a parenting class. As a result of the class, Ed and Julie decided to have family meetings so the girls could become part of the problem-solving process in the family.

Family Meetings Invite Cooperation and Encourage Horizontal Communication

Ed and Julie wanted to model cooperation and contribution in their family instead of control over others. In the past, sitting down with the kids meant telling them what to do. Ed and Julie knew they didn't want to do that anymore, but they didn't have any experience doing it any other way. They felt both excited and apprehensive, but decided the only way to learn was to start.

At the first meeting, Ed and Julie told their daughters, "We would like to have a meeting once a week with the whole family. We can help each other solve problems, plan family activities, and talk about things that are important to us. We'll keep a list in the kitchen during the week, and we can write down anything we'd like to talk about at the meeting. We'd like to have the meeting Sunday after lunch." The girls weren't sure what a meeting was, but they said, "OK."

The following Sunday, Ed and Julie sat at the table with the girls, turned off the TV, took the phone off the hook, and began.

"Let's start with appreciations or compliments and thank-yous. This is a chance for anyone at the table to tell someone else in the family something positive. Who would like to start?"

Mom said, "I'd like to thank Erica (the 8-year-old) for doing such a good job cleaning up the spill in the kitchen the other day."

Francesca, the 10-year-old, caught on immediately and said, "I'd like to thank Dad for driving me to my basketball game."

Not to be left out, Marilee, the 6-year-old said, "I want to thank my sisters for taking me to the park to play."

Then Dad read the list of items that had collected on the agenda. During the week, instead of trying to solve every problem as it came up, both parents had suggested to the girls, "Let's put it on the list for our meeting."

The list included what to do for fun as a family once a week; a complaint by Erica about Francesca "borrowing" her sister's sweater without asking; a suggestion by Francesca, the oldest, to stay up later; and a request from Marilee for help with a school project. Julie added another item on the list; she wanted help with the dishes after dinner.

Julie explained that they would set the timer for fifteen minutes and talk about the items on the list. If they didn't finish the entire list, that was OK. Any items that didn't get covered could wait until the next meeting. She told the girls they might want to talk about some items without trying to fix them. In other cases, they could help each other come up with a list of ideas for solving a problem (brainstorming) and pick the suggestion the family would like to try for one week.

As the family held more meetings, they found more to discuss: their calendars, money matters, and chores. They practiced emotional honesty (see Chapter 2) by communicating their feelings and learning to listen to each other without judging or criticizing.

At some meetings, family members stomped off angry; at others, someone cried or used a power play. Even though the family meetings weren't "perfect," compared to the closed system of communication before recovery, the progress was enormous. Julie and Ed were grateful for the healing that took place in their family through family meetings, emotional honesty, and the other ideas they learned in their parenting class.

Julie and Ed felt excited because the girls were being honest about their thoughts and feelings. The kids quickly discovered no one would tell them what to do or how to think. They learned their opinions were valued and important. Many issues that used to lead to fights and tears could now be listed on the agenda. After a cooling-off period (waiting until the meeting time), it was easier to be respectful when solving problems. Instead of threats and promises, the family members were all present simultaneously to work out agreements they were willing to live with for at least one week. If the agreement didn't work, they put the problem back on the agenda and worked on another solution.

In addition to family meetings and emotional honesty, many other communication skills can bring closeness to the family. Some families may feel hesitant about starting family meetings. They may feel more comfortable starting with other communication strategies. For Sherm, in our next story, the family meeting was too big a step from the closed system he grew up in and maintained as an adult. He felt more comfortable taking smaller steps.

Learning to Listen with Love Keeps Communication Horizontal and Encouraging

Sherm's mother was a closet alcoholic. At an ACoA (Adult Children of Alcoholics) meeting, he shared a memory from his preschool years that he said was typical of how people interacted in his family. He was at a funeral for another 3-year-old who was killed on his street. It was the only time as a small child that Sherm remembered seeing his mother cry. He reached up to hold his mother's hand, and she pulled away from him, wiped her eyes, and took on a stern expression.

As he watched that scene, Sherm made an unconscious decision. He decided that it was important to control pain and that it was wrong to show feelings or talk about painful events. As a parent, when things got painful or feelings started to surface in his family, he either controlled his feelings or tried to control the situation around him. He thought he could stop the hurting by taking charge of everything.

Sherm wanted to break the cycle of unhealthy communication he learned as a kid. He wasn't sure how to begin. He didn't have a picture of healthy communication from his childhood. Sherm did not want to take a parenting class, but felt comfortable reading books on parenting, communication skills, and relationships. Although he was anxious to make changes, he was afraid to express feelings or let others express theirs. In spite of his fear, Sherm decided to try three activities he found in the book *Together and Liking It* by Lynn Lott and Dru West: "Listening with Closed Lips," "The Three Yeses," and "What Is It About That...?"

Listening with Closed Lips

The "Listening with Closed Lips" lesson taught him that the only responses he could make while his daughter was talking were sounds he could make with his lips closed like, "Ummmmm. Umhmmm. Umm? Hmmm."

In his attempts to stop feelings from happening, Sherm had never listened to his daughter for fear of what she might say. He decided that listening with lips closed might invite her to talk and would help him learn more about her. Once Sherm decided listening was a priority, he found many opportunities to practice with his daughter.

Sherm's 13-year-old daughter, Franny, was a very angry child who frequently skipped school. The school counselor called regularly to report on problems at school. One of Franny's teachers sent notes home saying Franny never turned in her assignments. Sherm's usual way of handling Franny's school problems was to nag, lecture, scold, order, and threaten Franny. None of this was helping Franny succeed in school, and the communication between Sherm and Franny was going downhill fast.

Sherm decided he couldn't make things worse if he tried listening with closed lips. The book suggested that he start off the conversation with a question and then keep his lips together. It was OK to make comforting sounds, but the focus was on listening, not talking.

At dinner that night, Sherm told Franny he'd like to spend some time talking about school with her. Franny made a face and said uncooperatively, "Fine." She was sure she was in for one more lecture, but she was good at blocking her father out and not listening, so she figured she could pretend to listen one more time.

To her surprise, Sherm started the discussion by saying, "I'm sorry I have done so much talking and so little listening about school. I can tell you are unhappy about school. I would be interested in knowing what is going on for you."

When Franny said, "Yeah, sure!" in her defiant voice, Sherm kept his lips together and continued to listen.

There was silence, and then Franny continued, "You wouldn't believe anything I had to say anyway. You always take the teacher's side!"

Sherm kept his lips together, nodded his head, and continued to listen. Franny wasn't sure how to handle this. She waited for him to talk. When he didn't talk, but maintained eye contact and apparent interest in her, she continued.

"I hate school. The teachers pick on me. They like the kids who get good grades. They don't care about me, and I don't care about them."

Sherm touched Franny's shoulder and said, "I'm sorry it's so awful for you. Thank you for telling me more about school."

"No big deal," Franny said, and went to her room. Sherm thought he detected a small bounce in her step.

With a success under his belt, Sherm felt more confident to continue practicing his communication skills. He decided to practice each evening. After more practice listening with closed lips, Sherm was ready to try "The Three Yeses."

The Three Yeses

Sherm's job was to ask questions until he got three "yeses" from Franny, or positive responses to indicate she understood. The idea was to practice an attitude of curiosity with his daughter and to stay away from lectures and judgments.

When we are curious, we find out how our kids think and feel. Sometimes they tell us things we disagree with or may even dislike hearing. Listening to them doesn't mean we agree with them. It's respectful to hear their point of view and helpful to know how they see the world. People don't want to share personal information if they think the listener is going to judge or criticize. There are many activities to practice an attitude of curiosity, but "The Three Yeses" is helpful for beginners. Here is an example.

"Franny," said Sherm, "I'd like to clear up some confusion I have about what you've been telling me about school. Are you saying you want to drop out of school?"

By asking questions that start with "Are you saying..." Sherm can learn even more about how his daughter thinks and feels. He may even help her clarify some of her ideas in the process.

"Why would I want to drop out of school? All my friends are there! Just because I can't stand my teachers doesn't mean I don't want to go to school." Franny looked at her Dad with that "How can adults be such idiots?" expression.

"Are you saying you wish your teacher would care more about how you feel?"

"Yeah, that would be nice, but it's never gonna happen." (First yes.)

"Are you saying that you don't like to turn homework in to a person you don't respect?"

Franny looked up wide-eyed at her father and asked in amazement, "How did you know that?" (Second yes.)

"Just a guess, but I can understand that you don't feel like cooperating with people you don't think respect you."

"You can?" questioned Franny with teary eyes.

"Sure, I've often had those thoughts myself," said Sherm. "Are you also saying that unless the teacher changes, you're willing to flunk this class?"

"I guess so, even though I'm not really planning to flunk, but it seems like I'm going to if I don't turn in my homework." (Third yes.)

"Honey, I have some ideas about some things you might want to consider. Maybe sometime you'd be interested to hear what I have in mind."

Franny eyed her father suspiciously, expecting the old lectures to follow, but he remained silent. "Maybe I'd be interested in your ideas, Dad, but not tonight."

Sherm felt bad that Franny was willing to flunk a class but happy that he was establishing closeness and communication with his daughter. He decided to try another skill with her called "What Is It About That...?" to learn more about why she didn't want to hear his ideas. He decided to wait for another time, so Franny wouldn't feel pressured to listen to him when she didn't want to. As Sherm's skills grew, so did his respect both for his daughter and for himself.

"What Is It About That...?" Helps Clarify Thoughts and Feelings

This activity provides an opportunity to continue practicing an attitude of curiosity by asking, "What Is It About That...?" until the person gets clearer on what his or her issues are.

One night as Franny and Sherm were watching TV, Franny turned to her father and said, "Dad, I'm flunking my class and it's too late to do anything about it. I'm sorry I didn't listen to your ideas, but I just didn't want advice."

Sherm responded by turning off the TV and saying, "What is it about me giving advice that you don't like?"

"If you give advice, I think I have to do what you say."

"What is it about doing what I say that you don't like?"

"Dad, that's a dumb question! I'm almost 14, and I'm old enough to make up my own mind about stuff!"

"So if I give a suggestion, you think I'm telling you what to do and you'd rather decide for yourself?" asked Sherm.

"Didn't you feel that way when you were my age?"

"Sure," replied Sherm, "but I don't expect you to do what I say. I'd just like to share my ideas with you to consider along with whatever you have in mind. I might see some possibilities you don't see."

"Dad, at my age, I'd still think I'm supposed to do what you say."

"Franny, I'm not going to argue with you or try to make you change your mind. Sometime I hope you'll give us a chance to try it a different way."

"Let me think about it, Dad," she said, "and don't look so sad. It'll be OK. I can take my class over in summer school. All my friends will be there." Franny gave her dad a big grin and turned on the TV.

Sherm couldn't believe how good it felt to communicate. He thought about all those years he had feared getting close because it would be too painful, and breathed a sigh of relief that he wasn't wasting any more time with his daughter.

Julie, Ed, and Sherm found ways to open communication. As families continue to heal and practice horizontal communication, they are ready for conflict resolution skills that require mutual respect.

Conflict Resolution Skills That Really Work

Resolving conflicts in a respectful, horizontal way brings about closeness and open communication in the family. Resolving conflicts with vertical communication increases distance and isolation. To improve the family atmosphere, we recommend horizontal communication skills. These include action instead of words, limited choices, deciding what you will do, asking for what you want, joint problem solving, and brainstorming.

In the Kramer family, the substance of abuse was work. Vince Kramer spent every waking moment at the office. He left early in the morning and came home after the kids were in bed each night. The Kramers had three children under age 7, and Gina Kramer was a nervous wreck. She felt overwhelmed and abandoned. Her idea of having children didn't mean she would do it all herself—she was living with an absent other.

Vince Kramer ignored Gina's demands and pleas for help. He told her that it was her job to handle the kids and that if she were more organized, everything would be fine. Gina couldn't think of any convincing arguments, but she felt terrible and alone. She kept waiting for Vince to change so things would get better.

Finally Gina realized that talking wasn't making anything better. But she didn't know about nonverbal communication. It never occurred to her that she could act instead of talk, and could decide what *she* would do instead of trying to change what *he* did.

One day, while watching a daytime talk show, Gina heard a guest talk about co-dependence. The woman, a young mother like Gina, commented that it had finally occurred to her that the only person who was going to change was herself. She stopped waiting for her husband to fix things when she realized he was the *last* person who cared about changes. Gina listened with interest to find out what the woman had done.

The young woman commented that her first step involved acting instead of talking. She decided to give herself a break from the kids once a day. Instead of hoping her husband would find extra money in the budget to help with baby-sitters, she hired the 10-year-old next door to come play with the kids while she took a nap. She paid the baby-sitter out of the grocery money.

Gina thought, "I could do that. Even if we ate macaroni and cheese three times a week, it would be worth it." Within the week, Gina found a sixth-grader in her neighborhood who wanted to earn some extra money. While Gina soaked in the tub and read a book for an hour each day, the neighbor kid played board games with her children. The kids loved the attention, and Gina loved the break. Gina discovered the power of nonverbal communication, of using action instead of words.

Gina also learned from the talk show program that it was helpful to resolve conflicts with the kids by giving them limited choices. The next time they squabbled underfoot, Gina said, "Would you like to stay in the kitchen and play quietly without fighting, or go in the living room where you can continue your squabbling?"

When the kids didn't respond, Gina said, "No choice is the same as the living room. You can come back in the kitchen and try again in fifteen minutes." Then Gina practiced acting without talking: she took the kids by the hand and led them to the living room. When one of them crept back into the kitchen, she firmly but kindly took her hand and led her back to the living room without any words. (Keeping your lips pressed together helps with this.)

Ask for What We Want

As Gina felt more courageous, she realized she could ask for what she wanted. At first Gina expected Vince to read her mind. But that wasn't happening, so Gina decided to be more direct. "After all," she told herself, "it couldn't get any worse than it already is."

Gina said to Vince one evening, "I want a break from the kids each week. I would prefer that they spend time with you, but I'd be happy with extra money to hire a baby-sitter. If money is a problem, perhaps you could drop them at your parents' house one afternoon on the weekend."

Vince refused to help Gina get what she wanted, but she felt better getting her needs out on the table. Just because you ask for what you want doesn't mean you'll get it. You can be sure that if you *don't* ask, however, no one can read your mind.

When she made her request, Gina became more aware of how resistant Vince was. She hadn't really expected much participation from him with the kids. But hearing him say clearly, "I'm not going to help you," left Gina with no doubts as to where he stood.

It takes two people to jointly solve problems in a family. Gina would have preferred to work things out with Vince, but as he was unwilling she couldn't force him. She can always decide what she will do and use action, not words. When at least two people in a family are willing to work together, it is possible to work things out through joint problem-solving skills. Here are the six steps to use.

Six Steps for Joint Problem Solving

1. State your observation of a problem and what you would like: "I notice _____, and I'd like us to work out another way to handle this that we both can live with. I'd like us to agree to take each other seriously and not attack or hurt each other."

2. Ask others involved how they view the problem and how they feel about it. Then feed back what they say to let them know you heard, or to invite their correction if you didn't hear what they meant.

3. State your feelings and views of the problem. Ask them to feed back what you said. Give appreci-

111

ations to your partner or children for listening and understanding.

4. Ask first, "Have you thought of something else you might do?" If not, brainstorm alternatives together, or pretend you have a magic wand and create options.

5. Choose an alternative that you can all agree to try for a short time (one day, one week, and so on). Role-play the chosen alternative if possible.

6. Agree on a review date to see how things went during the trial period, and thank the others involved.

Gina decided to try joint problem solving with Vince. That night she met Vince at the door as he came home from work and said, "Vince, I have something I'd like to talk to you about. Let's sit down and have dinner together so we can talk."

Vince said, "I don't want to get into anything heavy. I've had a hard day at work."

"Well, there's something important that I want to talk to you about," replied Gina seriously.

"If this is more ways that I'm supposed to help with the kids, forget it!"

"Vince, I can't make you talk with me, but I need your help. I can't handle this all myself anymore. I'm overwhelmed and scared. I feel like I'm falling apart."

"What do you want from me?" asked Vince.

Step 1 in Joint Problem Solving

Gina began with the first step in problem solving. She said, "Vince, I'd like your help to come up with something that will work for both of us. I know you're tired when you come home from work, but I need a break from the kids. I notice you seem to resent it when I ask for help, and I'd like to know more about that. I'd like to work out a deal with you that we talk about what is going on between us without attacking or hurting each other. I'd like it if we took each other seriously."

"I don't mean to attack you," said Vince, "but I get so angry when you don't listen to what I tell you. I'm willing to agree to talk without attacking and hurting if you are."

"Good. I can make that agreement," said Gina.

Step 2 in Joint Problem Solving

Now Gina said, "I would like to listen and hear you. Let's try again."

Vince said, "I work hard all day and deserve to be able to come home and have some peace and quiet and time to myself."

"So you're saying that you're exhausted and evenings are your time to recover by having time alone."

"You got it. Don't I provide for this family? You have everything you want!"

"You feel angry because I'm making demands when you do so much for us."

"Yeah, that's what I've been trying to tell you all these years!"

Step 3 in Joint Problem Solving

Then Gina asked, "Are you willing to hear what my issues are?"

Vince said, "What?"

"I'm with the kids all day, and even though I love them, they're very demanding and wear me out. I feel alone and scared about having all the responsibility of dealing with the kids."

"What do you want me to do?" asked Vince.

"It would help if I thought you understood my feelings."

"I can see it's difficult, but you're the one who wanted kids."

"You sound angry with me for having children. Do you wish we *didn't* have the kids?"

"Of course not. But I do so much already."

"You didn't hear what I'm feeling. You don't have to fix it, but I wish you could let me know that you understand how alone and scared and overwhelmed I feel."

Reluctantly, Vince said, "Yeah, I hear you feel overwhelmed and scared and think you have to do it all yourself."

"Thanks, Vince. I know you don't see it the same way, and that's OK."

Step 4 in Joint Problem Solving

Next Gina asked, "Would you be willing to help me think of something else we could do that would work for both of us?"

Vince asked, "What do you have in mind?"

Gina said, "I'm not sure, but maybe we could think of some ideas that would fit both of our needs. We could make a list and see if there's something we could both try out for a short time. Maybe we could try something for a week. Let's brainstorm and see how many possibilities we can come up with."

Gina started: "One idea is that you could take the kids to McDonald's and the park for an hour on Saturday or Sunday. Another idea I have is that you could come home a half hour earlier and read the kids a story before they go to sleep."

Vince said, "Why don't I drop them at your parents' one afternoon this weekend?"

Gina said, "Let's add that idea to the list. Another idea is that we could set up a baby-sitter kitty and use the money for me to get a sitter."

Vince suggested, "Maybe we could leave the kids with a sitter and go to breakfast together Sunday morning."

Step 5 in Joint Problem Solving

"Is there one thing on the list we could try out this week?" asked Gina.

Vince said, "I'd like to leave the kids with a sitter and go to breakfast with you Sunday morning."

Gina replied, "That isn't my first choice, but I would be willing to try that out."

Vince asked, "What's your first choice?"

Gina said, "I would prefer a choice where you spend some time with the kids because I think they would enjoy being with you. If you took them out of the house, I would have a chance to catch up around here without constant distractions from the kids."

Vince said, "Gina, I can see how that would work best for you, but I'm not ready to take that on. Let's start with you and me going out to breakfast this week and see how that works."

Step 6 in Joint Problem Solving

Gina replied, "OK, and then let's get together next Monday and re-evaluate our plan."

"Thanks for being flexible and understanding, Gina," volunteered Vince.

"Thanks for working with me, Vince."

As you can see, effective communication skills do not provide a cure-all. They do help create closer relationships and help people know who they are, what they feel, and what they want. Effective communication ends isolation and loneliness and helps people work on solutions and agreements while maintaining dignity and respect for all concerned.

Communicate with Kids About Drugs

Recovering parents know firsthand the realities and dangers of using drugs and alcohol. The last thing you want is for your kids to go through the living hell that you went through. You want to break the cycle of addiction.

The pressure of that responsibility and the fear that your kids are at risk could motivate you to overreact in counterproductive ways. You may be tempted to make sure your kids don't even start using drugs by employing parenting methods that are extremely controlling. But the more you attempt to control your kids, the less effective you are. It is equally ineffective to ignore or neglect dealing with your kids about drugs. Going into denial and pretending drugs don't exist is more devastating to young people than any overreactive control measures you might take.

The Four Essentials for Effective Communication About Drugs

You can help your kids learn about drugs and their uses and possible abuses through communication that is honest, informative, open, and nonjudgmental.

1. By *honest*, we mean "telling it like it is." If you have a feeling or a belief, it is important to share it as your *opinion*, but not as the only way to look at things. (You might want to review Chapter 2, on emotional honesty, at this point.)

   Some parents hesitate to talk about their own problems with drugs for fear that it will lower the kids' opinion of them or give the kids ideas. We've discovered that honesty opens up real communication. Kids don't have to worry about or try to hide their own imperfections when they know their parents are real people who have made their share of mistakes.

2. The word *informative* means that the information shared is accurate and not just an opinion. Telling kids that if they try drugs they'll become addicts (or other such threats) is a way of losing credibility. The first time kids try drugs and nothing bad happens, they often decide their parents don't know what they are talking about. Scare tactics with kids may be effective to stop them from using drugs when they are young, but once kids become preadolescents or teenagers, scare tactics have the opposite effect. Some kids feel obligated to prove how "stupid" and "wrong" adults are. When kids get accurate information, it helps them consider the choices they are making and what the possible consequences of their choices might be.

3. The phrase *open communication* means that you invite discussion as opposed to shutting it off. People to whom others feel comfortable talking are usually noncritical and noncontrolling. They seem to care what others think, even if they don't see it the same way. They feel free to tell others their own opinion without expecting others to do things their way.

4. By *nonjudgmental*, we mean not seeing issues as "right" or "wrong." Nothing closes down communication quicker than talking to someone who always has to be right. No one likes to be told he or she is wrong or stupid. It helps curb your judgmental tendencies when you ask questions from sincere curiosity and then listen to draw your kids out about what they think.

You cannot stop your kids from trying drugs, or even from abusing them, if that is what they decide to do. What you can do is practice honesty, equip your kids with accurate information about drugs, keep the doors of communication open by letting your kids know your love for them is unconditional, and remain nonjudgmental by creating a relationship where your kids feel safe to talk to you and get your input about their choices. When you abstain from judgments, your kids know that if they get into an abusive situation with their own experimentation, you will be there with honesty, love, and support that is empowering instead of enabling.

You cannot provide a script of exactly what to say when talking to kids about drugs. The important thing is to establish a close relationship where there are opportunities for continued dialogue and growth. It is much easier to establish close relationships when you understand about separate realities.[1]

Separate Realities

We have stressed many times in this book that it's not only what happens to people that is important but also what they decide about it. Separate realities explain why each person involved in a situation may interpret the situation differently and make different decisions. The separate reality of each of your kids will affect his or her separate decision about drugs.

Why Kids Use Drugs and Why Kids Don't—It's a Decision

It is very easy for people to get caught up in the belief that if they only say or do the right thing as adults, they can save their kids from any problems with drugs or alcohol. Often people assume their kids think about things the same way they do. They don't check with their kids to find out what the kids are *actually* deciding about what is presented to them.

Parents are always giving messages, both verbal and nonverbal, and kids are always making decisions, both conscious and unconscious. When you are aware of this process, you can ask yourself, "What am I saying to my

---

[1]Jane Nelsen gives a thorough explanation of separate realities in her book *Understanding: Eliminating Stress and Finding Serenity in Life and Relationships* (Rocklin, CA: Prima, 1988).

kids, and what are they deciding about it?" As you read through this section, it will become clear there is no guarantee that kids will decide what parents hope or assume they will.

The following stories show how several parents communicated with their kids about drugs and the decisions the kids made. When you read the stories, notice that there are always two parts to the communication process: (1) what is said and (2) what is decided about what is said.

For years, Marnie was addicted to cocaine and alcohol. She decided to enter a drug treatment program to deal with her addictions. Marnie came out of treatment free of drugs and inspired to work on her recovery. She also wanted to share with her teenage son what she had learned about addiction, in hopes that he wouldn't have to go through the pain she had gone through.

Marnie told her son Noah that he was at risk because she was an alcoholic. She explained that research shows the risk of becoming an addict is increased depending on how many people in the family have a drug problem. She told Noah that because of her family history it was possible that he had a genetic predisposition to become an addict. She encouraged Noah for these reasons not to use chemicals. She invited him to get active in Alateen and to read the literature she brought home from her AA meetings.

Noah listened intently, thanked his mom for her help, and even read and discussed the literature she gave him. As far as his mother knew, her approach was successful. Noah acted like all their discussions made a difference. He presented the picture he thought his mom wanted to see.

However, even though Marnie was honest, informative, open, and nonjudgmental, Noah was more influenced by his Uncle Les's nonverbal communication. Noah's father had died when Noah was 2 years old. Les became Noah's male role model and spent a lot of time with Noah. Les used marijuana daily. He didn't hide his use, but smoked marijuana as if it were a regular cigarette. Les was "macho," rebellious, and reckless.

Les and Noah had a loving relationship and spent a lot of time doing "male" activities together. They liked to race boats, drive fast cars, and jet ski. The nonverbal communication conveyed that boys will be boys, that they're wild and like to have fun, and that it's OK as long as they hide it from the "little woman."

Then Noah joined the army and was stationed far away from his mom. After basic training, he began to abuse alcohol daily. When his friends expressed concern about his drunk driving, he told them he could do as he pleased and no one could tell him what to do. Noah thought that he was invincible and that nothing could happen to him, because he was "macho" like his uncle. Noah found a group of guys who shared his lifestyle and established a routine of heavy drinking and drugging. Of course, he hid all this from his mother, who was under the illusion that he was too smart to abuse drugs because she had told him about the risk factors.

The *verbal* message Noah heard was that drugs are dangerous for him and that he was at risk. The *nonverbal* message was that men can do risky things and nothing will happen to them, but they need to keep that behavior separate from the women in their lives. Noah decided that he could do what he wanted, that he was immune to adverse consequences, and that women need to be told what they want to hear.

In the Clark family, the kids didn't get mixed messages, as Noah did. However, Charlie, the father in this family, was opinionated and judgmental. This invited the kids to agree or to take opposite positions instead of thinking for themselves. Charlie Clark repeatedly told his kids it was stupid to use alcohol. He told stories from his days as a bartender about people who got drunk and acted stupid. One of his favorite stories was about the customer who got drunk, got into a fight with a policeman, and bit the policeman's ear off.

Charlie followed his own advice about alcohol. The Clarks didn't drink or even keep alcohol in their home. Both the verbal and nonverbal messages in the Clark family were that it was stupid to use drugs.

Charlie's oldest daughter, Dorie, decided that her father was right, and she refused to use alcohol or hang out with kids who did. When Dorie found her best friend with a bottle of vodka in her car, she decided she could no longer hang out with anyone who would do something so "stupid."

But Dorie's sister, Pat, rebelled against the family values and used nearly every drug she could find. She hid her drug use from the family. Pat hung out with a group of kids who experimented and rebelled against the conventional wisdom. They avoided alcohol, however, because they didn't want to be like those "stupid" adults around them. They saw any *other* drug as mind expanding and consciousness raising.

(An interesting sequel to this story is that as adults, they changed their decisions. Dorie became a regular user of alcohol, and Pat refused to use any drug stronger than vitamin C. She had learned from the consequences of her behavior.)

In addition to increasing their awareness about what their kids are deciding about what they tell adults, parents must also consider the age-appropriateness of their own communication. Kids are ready for different levels of information and sophistication at different ages. Parents can't use the same language with a preschooler as with a budding adolescent. They need to speak kids' language and use examples they can understand, because the examples relate to the kids' lives.

Many parents have asked, "What do I say to my 4-year-old about drugs? How do I talk to my teenager about drugs? If I tell my kids not to use drugs, is that enough?" Because we know how difficult it is to talk to kids about drugs with honesty, information, openness, and a nonjudgmental attitude, we're including sample dialogues by age group to help answer those and other questions.

In the following dialogues, some of the parents followed our four guidelines of honesty, information, openness, and a nonjudgmental attitude. Others did not. Notice the varying results of their choices.

Talking to Preschool Children About Drugs

The first time toddlers get sick and need medicine can be the beginning of their "drug education." The following dialogue demonstrates how a parent can use this opportunity to teach some important messages about drugs.

Toddler: (with runny nose and flushed cheeks) Owwie, Mommy. My throat hurts.

Mom: Let's take your temperature and see if you have a fever. You look sick to me. (Looks at thermometer.) Yup, you have a fever, and we need to get your fever down. We'll get you a children's aspirin and a glass of orange juice for your hurt throat. Then we'll sit on the couch and read stories together so you can rest. When we don't feel well, there are a lot of different things we can do to feel better. Sometimes we need an aspirin, sometimes a nap, and sometimes we might need to check with the doctor. We'll check your temperature later to see how you're doing.

Toddler: Can I have a lot of ice in my orange juice, Mommy?

Mom: Sure, sweetie. Now let's go to the cabinet and get you an aspirin. Remember, aspirin is something moms get if their little girls and boys need them, and not something for you to take by yourself. Too many aspirins could make you very sick. That's why we keep them in a safe place.

This mother is beginning to give information about drugs. She not saying drugs will make you better or that drugs are the only way to fix a problem. She doesn't want to start her child in the habit of thinking that pills are the only answer. She assures her child they can help, but too many could be dangerous. The important thing is to teach kids that there are some drugs (medication) that may help us get better, and that there are many ways we can heal that do not call for drugs.

At the same time, it's important for parents to watch their chemical intake and model what they say. At this age, kids are great observers and copy what parents do. If Mom or Dad take a nap or walk to feel better as opposed to taking a pill, the child registers that message.

Talking to Toddlers About Family Members Who Abuse Drugs

We may need to talk to preschoolers about relatives who are acting different because they are drunk or under the influence of a drug. Instead of saying things like "Grandma is sick today" or "Daddy doesn't feel well," it is important to be honest and use words that say what *is* happening.

Four-year-old: Why does Grandma act so funny when we visit?

Dad: Grandma has had too much alcohol to drink, and she is drunk. Sometimes people do things that are not good for them, and Grandma is doing that right now. Are you scared of Grandma?

Four-year-old: I think Grandma is funny.

Dad: Grandma may be acting funny, but it's not healthy for Grandma to drink so much, and I wish she wouldn't do that.

As children get older and spend more time away from the family, there are some new messages about drugs we want to make sure they get.

Talking to Children Aged 5 to 10 About Drugs

The 5 to 10 age group needs preparation for what could happen to them when they are "out in the world" away from their families. Parents can encourage them to question information and think about what they are doing instead of just going along. At this age, kids usually think in black-and-white terms, tend to agree with adult warnings, and become very opinionated about warnings they have accepted. You help prepare them for the future when you create open communication by asking questions that help them learn *how* to think instead of telling them *what* to think.

Many kids are approached to use drugs at school in the primary grades. Even at this early age, they may be encouraged to try or buy drugs. Kids need skills to deal with people who tell them drugs are good for them. Role-playing is a fun way to teach skills. Ask kids to think of some things they could do or say when they are approached to try or buy drugs. Then role-play with them so they can practice their ideas.

Sample Dialogue with a 9-Year-Old

Here's a sample of how to talk to a child about drugs at school.

Mom: I got the school paper, and there was an article about some kids who were caught selling drugs at your school. Are you aware of that?

Son: Yeah, Mom. Kids are always trying to get us to buy stuff.

Mom: Has anyone ever approached you?

Son: Sure, but I say, "No way!"

Mom: I'm really glad to hear that. I feel sad and scared to think that you have to deal with that at your age. What do you think about drugs?

Son: I think they're stupid, and I'm never going to take any. One of our teachers told us about a kid who licked some stickers and they had PCP on them. The kid almost died. I don't want anything like that to happen to me.

Mom: I'm sorry, honey, that there are people in the world who would try to talk you into doing something dangerous for you, but I'm so glad to know you care enough about yourself not to risk hurting yourself. I feel much better now that we've talked.

Look for the Teaching Moments

You can encourage open communication with kids in this age-5-to-10 group by helping them question media messages. Dicuss TV commercials and other advertising with them—sometimes it helps just to bring to their conscious awareness how they are being bombarded with "Do drug" messages.

Dialogue with a 7-Year-Old

A parent was watching TV with his son one night. Every commercial was for some kind of sleep, cold, fever, or pain remedy, not to mention beer. Dad noticed his son humming the catchy tunes and repeating the dialogue. He started to think about how much TV his son watched and how unconscious his son was about the messages he was getting. He decided to talk about this.

Dad: I notice you've memorized all the commercials. Do you ever think about what they are saying?

Son: What do you mean, Dad?

Dad: While I've been sitting here with you, we've had about twenty people tell us if we can't sleep or have a sniffle, an ache, or a pain, we should take some kind of a pill. Even the beer commercials are telling us that if we drink beer we'll have more friends, have fun, look good, and enjoy life more. I feel angry when I listen to this.

Son: Why are you angry, Dad?

Dad: Because I think you might believe all this stuff, instead of realizing that this is an ad designed to talk people into buying things. I don't think we have to take a pill if we can't sleep. Sometimes we have a lot on our minds, or we're just not tired and that's OK. We'll probably catch up on our sleep another night if we are tired enough. And the people I see who drink beer act rude and impolite. Some of them don't know how to have any fun unless they get high. We don't need to drink to have fun.

Son: Dad, I don't believe all that stuff on TV.

Dad: I'm glad to hear that, but I really want you to start thinking about what you are hearing and remember that commercials are meant to get people to buy things and not necessarily help people feel better.

You also have opportunities to practice honesty by talking about your own drug use or that of another parent. The more you use drug-specific language (such as "pot," "crack," "loaded," or "wasted") the more prepared your children are to make sense out of what's happening in their world, as the following story shows.

Kids this age can be extremely curious and open to learning. In the following dialogue—which might seem very scary to some of you reading this book—an 8- and a 10-year-old demonstrated their curiosity and ended up with a lot of information about drugs.

Honesty Satisfies Curiosity

Zoe, age 8, and Christopher, age 10, had just completed a unit on drugs at school. Coincidentally, their Aunt Joanne came to visit from back East. The kids knew she had taken a lot of drugs in the 1960s and they wanted to ask her all about her experiences. They wanted to know what Joanne took, how it felt, what was the effect, whether she still used drugs, and if not, why and how did she stop.

Joanne answered their questions honestly and didn't glorify or downgrade her experience. It was clear that she was speaking about how it was for her, not how it was for everyone. Joanne practiced honesty and openness while giving a lot of information in a non-judgmental way.

Joanne: I'm surprised that you kids are asking these questions, because you're so young. Do people talk about drugs in your school?

Christopher: Yeah, kids use drugs in our school. Sometimes they try to give us drugs or sell them.

Joanne: What kind of drugs are kids giving you?

129

Christopher: Lots of kids smoke marijuana, and sometimes they have PCP. One kid in our school has a lot of different kinds of pills to try. Did you use any of those drugs?

Joanne: I used marijuana, hash, speed, acid, and mushrooms.

Zoe: What does it feel like to get high on marijuana?

Joanne: For me, marijuana heightened my awareness, but it also made me tired. I always got hungry and felt like I wanted to eat. It was strange in a way, because when I was high on marijuana I had a clearer perspective, but at the same time, it slowed me down a lot. When I first started using marijuana, I spent a lot of time talking about my new awareness and how different things were.

Zoe: Where did you get marijuana, Aunt Joanne?

Joanne: In the 1960s it was easy. My friends brought it back from California. Later some of them started saving the seeds and grew their own marijuana. Some of my friends traveled to Mexico, Afghanistan, and Turkey and they brought the drug back from those places.

Christopher: Where did you use it?

Joanne: I'm a very social person, and I only used drugs in social situations, like at parties. Everyone in our generation disapproved of alcohol, and we all thought marijuana was better than alcohol. We saw it as a consciousness-raising, mind-expanding thing. My friends never got addicted, but lot of people did.

Zoe: Do you still use it, or have you stopped?

Joanne: I don't use drugs anymore. I used marijuana off and on all through college and a few years after college, but only occasionally. If I was at a party and someone had some, I would have a little. We would share a joint between four or five people. I had a rule for myself that I would never spend money on drugs, so the only time

I tried them was if someone else had them. After a while, drugs got more expensive and harder to find. People started buying drugs from strangers, and we weren't sure what was mixed in with the marijuana. That got scary, because some people would mix marijuana with dangerous materials to make it look like more. The drug didn't work the same, either, when it was less pure.

Christopher: Is that why you stopped?

Joanne: I got tired of it. You don't get the same experience after you use a drug for a while. I built up tolerance and had to smoke too much to get high, and still didn't feel as good as it did at first. I realized it was a waste of time to sit around smoking dope, so I quit. I wanted to enjoy life. I knew people who started using marijuana for a different reason. They didn't want to feel their feelings. They started using the drug all the time to avoid feeling. They stopped dealing with their problems and used drugs instead. I never used drugs for that reason.

Zoe: Why did you use drugs?

Joanne: All the drugs I used were to expand my mind and create a different consciousness. My use was only experimental. When I was done experimenting, that was it for me.

Christopher: Did you ever get addicted to any of the drugs you used? In school they tell us that drugs are dangerous because we might start off experimenting and then get addicted.

Joanne: I think what leads to addiction is denial of your feelings and lack of information. The only drug I ever became hooked on was tobacco. I never had a fear I would be hooked on any other drug because I knew the other drugs were addictive, so I used them socially or experimentally, but never regularly. I didn't know tobacco was addictive, so I didn't pay attention to how many cigarettes I smoked. Before I knew it, I was hooked.

Joanne went on to answer the kids' questions about other drug use with the same style of openness and honesty. When they asked her if she knew anyone who was an addict, Joanne continued, "I have a friend who became addicted to hash and alcohol. He wanted to slow down and numb out. I hated those drugs for the same reasons he liked them.

"The one drug none of us ever wanted to use was heroin. I think that was partly because you used a needle and put the drug straight into your bloodstream. Also, we believe it was highly addictive. When you start getting into drugs, you hear about heroin and all the horror stories, how expensive it is, how people sell everything they have, and lose their dignity and self-respect. We heard these stories from people who used drugs, so because they were saying it's dangerous, we believed them."

Christopher: Our teacher told us that if we used cocaine only one time, we would be addicted. Do you think that's true, Aunt Joanne?

Joanne: The people I know who have become addicted have a desperation. They are looking for something to take away the pain and stop feeling. I suppose some could get addicted after using one time, but that's not the way it usually happens. I was never afraid of an addiction because I never wanted more than an adventure and a new experience. How about if we go out for a walk? That's about it for me on drugs for one day.

Zoe and Christopher said, "Thanks, Aunt Joanne. That was really interesting."

Christopher and Zoe didn't run out and experiment with drugs. Neither of them had any interest in using drugs, just a lot of curiosity for information about them. We can only guess at what they were deciding about what was presented to them.

As they grew up, Zoe went through a period of experimentation and social use of drugs. Christopher's approach seemed to be more of an all or nothing style. As a teen, he used marijuana daily for a summer and then stopped completely. In college, he experimented with alcohol for a few weeks and then decided it was more fun to go to classes alert than hung over. So he quit drinking large quantities of alcohol, but enjoyed trying out foreign beer on occasion.

We have talked to many kids who said they made better decisions when they were given honest information. They tell us they discount adults who are moralistic and make statements the kids don't believe. As one teenager said, "Why should we believe adults who told us we would get sick if we didn't eat our vegetables? We learned to discount those statements. We tend to discount most of the things they say about drugs, too."

Talking to Early Adolescents Aged 11 to 14

With kids aged 11 to 14, it is even more important to communicate by asking instead of telling. Kids this age do not respond well to orders. In fact, if you would like to *invite* your kids to use drugs, you might just as well tell them, "Don't do drugs! If I find out you have, you'll be grounded." Too many adolescents see such a statement as an invitation to a power struggle where the only choice is to win or to lose. They want to win without getting punished. They go "underground" so they won't get grounded.

At this age, nonjudgmental communication works best. One young teenage girl, who was sent to therapy because of her drug use, told her counselor, "Sometimes adults act so stupid. You would think they *want* kids to use drugs! They're always telling us, 'Don't do drugs!' Don't they know that only makes us want to do them more?"

Her counselor asked, "What would you recommend that parents who are worried about drugs tell their kids?"

She responded without hesitation: "I wish they would have told me that drugs could be dangerous and that they could hurt me. That would have helped a lot more."

Her counselor asked, "Didn't they tell you that?"

She looked surprised and said, "Yes, but it sounded more like a threat than information."

Overreacting from fear is not helpful to kids. The next story shows how Art's fears, based on his past drug experience, drove a wedge between him and his daughter. Art was unable to trust her because he was so sure she was out doing what he used to do at her age. He made a mistaken assumption that his daughter was exactly the same as he was as a teen.

Art went into recovery when his daughter Kim was 9 years old. Kim attended Alateen meetings and learned a lot about chemical abuse. At this age, she became clear that she was never going to use mood-altering chemicals.

Art was comfortable talking to his daughter about his using days and about his recovery and felt certain that Kim would never want to use chemicals. This began to change when Kim entered junior high. Art started to feel scared. Kim was in a larger world now. She was making new friends and getting involved in school activities.

Art started to lose faith in his daughter and act out his scared feelings. He questioned Kim about what she was doing and who she was seeing. At first Kim told her dad about her new friends. When he began criticizing them and suggesting that she not hang out with them, Kim began closing down and talked only if she were pressed.

Art felt Kim pulling away. This scared him even more, so he questioned her more. One day Kim was late coming home from school. When she walked in the door, Art began his harangue: "Where have you been? Let me look at your eyes. Have you been smoking pot?"

What are you talking about?" his daughter asked. "Will you get off my back? I told you I don't smoke pot! I probably *should,* since you already think I do!"

"I *know* those kids you hang out with smoke pot! Several people have seen them," her dad retorted.

"Just leave me alone," Kim screamed and ran to her room and slammed the door.

Art wasn't respectful of his daughter. But he didn't like what was happening and decided to get help. He found a counselor who was knowledgeable about drugs and teenagers. When he learned more about drug use, Art learned to maintain respect and act responsibly instead of fearfully with Kim.

Not everyone who uses drugs becomes dependent. Some kids may choose abstinence. Others may choose to experiment with drugs to see what they are like. Some kids use drugs socially, but would never consider using drugs on a regular basis.

Signs of Dangerous Drug Use

When drug use becomes a regular or daily pattern, kids are inviting serious problems. They are into problem use when they use drugs and their use creates difficulties in their lives. Instead of stopping, they use more. These kids are trying to change their feelings and solve their problems with chemicals. They need help to break this pattern.

Not all kids who get into problem use become addicted. Addiction occurs when a chemical becomes their primary relationship. They are willing to suffer any loss (school, family, job) except their drug of choice. When your kids show signs of problem use or chemical dependency, you need to reach out for help.

Not all parents of preadolescents have to deal with serious problems, although some act as though any mild use and brief experimentation were serious. At some point, however, most parents are presented with opportunities to deal with the "party" issue. With preadolescents, it is helpful to ask questions to get them to think about consequences, instead of telling them what will happen.

Help Kids Think Things Through by Asking Instead of Telling

In the next dialogue, a father helps his son explore the possible consequences of planning a party without adult supervision while his parents are out of town. Notice that the father is using questions to help his son consider different possibilities.

Son: Hey, Dad, are you guys going away this weekend?

Dad: Yes, Mom and I thought we'd leave you and your sister home and we'd head to the coast for an overnight. We need some time together.

Son: Can we have a party while you're gone?

Dad: I don't think that would be a good idea. We would feel comfortable if you have a party when we're in town, but not when we're away.

Son: Oh, that's tight! My friends don't want a bunch of parents around.

Dad: Mom and I aren't a bunch of parents, and I'm sure we can be discreet and well behaved if you have your friends over. Let me ask you some questions. Have you thought of what might happen if word gets out that we're out of town and you're having a party?

Son: We'd only let kids come who we know.

Dad: And what would you do if a lot of strange kids showed up and decided to crash the party?

Son: We'd ask them to leave.

Dad: And what if they said no?

Son: We'd call the police.

Dad: And what would you do in the meantime if they were in the house and destroying property or throwing up on things?

Son: We'd clean up and fix things after they left.

Dad: It sounds like you have a lot of ideas of how you would take care of the situation, but I don't think it's well thought through. If you can come up with some other ideas that would convince me that the situation wouldn't get out of hand, I'd be willing to continue this discussion. Otherwise, the answer is no.

Sometimes parents get angry with their kids because the kids don't think through consequences. But parents need to help them do that, by asking questions. When parents are critical or tell kids what the consequences will be, they alienate the kids. It is better to help them build thinking skills by inviting them to think things through. It's OK to tell kids no until you come up with something that is satisfactory to all involved. When you approach your kids with respect and openness, you may find a way to set up a win-win situation.

Teens' Need for Privacy

Preadolescents have already reached the age where they think they know everything, so now it is best to stop giving orders and start sharing feelings. It's OK to tell kids you probably won't agree or see things the same way, but that you won't punish them for honesty or differing opinions.

One 14-year-old said it very well in a counseling session one day. His mom was asking why he never talks to her anymore. He looked at her and said, "I wish I could talk to you, but you'd be mad and I might get in trouble."

Mom was surprised. She said, "Don't we have a deal that even if I get upset, you'll never get in trouble for telling the truth?"

"Yeah," he said, "but I'm afraid if I told you some of the things I'm planning to do, you'd change your mind."

Mom replied, "I wish you would trust me to keep my word so I could be your friend and confidante."

Even in the best relationships, it's still difficult for kids this age to communicate honestly with their parents. Even when parents demonstrate unconditional love, kids have their own beliefs about not wanting to upset or disappoint their parents. We can encourage them (instead of feeling jealous) to have other adult friends they can talk to, whom they know won't snitch on them or judge them.

Parents who take a controlling, "I know best, I'm right" attitude tend to lose all influence. Parents are even less help when they act as if everything is fine and when they handle the issue of drugs by closing their eyes and ignoring the situation. Kids feel scared and abandoned if their parents completely refuse to deal with the situation.

Heart-to-heart and gut-level honest communication is the best path with teens. This is especially true as kids get older. When you focus on preparing your preteens and teens to protect themselves instead of protecting them, you have a lot of influence. This is modeled in the dialogues that follow between parents and teens.

Talking with Teens About Drugs

Teenagers are not kids anymore, but they're not adults, either. Talking with them about drugs requires respect and clarity. In their book *I'm on Your Side: Resolving Conflict with Your Teenage Son or Daughter* (Rocklin, CA: Prima, 1991), Jane Nelson and Lynn Lott include a chapter on talking to teens about drugs. We recommend reading that chapter in addition to the information contained here.

We have found that a "Just say no" approach is ineffective and disrespectful at this age because it doesn't teach kids to think. Teenagers tell us the "Just say no" approach helped in elementary school, but that they laugh at it now. Honesty, openness, a nonjudgmental attitude, and sharing information go a lot farther with teenagers, as the following example shows.

Frank and Emily met while in recovery, married, and had a son, Randy. When Randy was born, Frank and Emily agreed to be open and honest about their past chemical abuse. They believed Randy would be at greater risk than other kids to become an addict or to marry one, and they wanted him to be prepared for whatever might happen. They both worked their programs, went to meetings, read and shared, had friends in recovery around, and took Randy to meetings.

Randy grew up knowing the language, symptoms, and dangers of chemical abuse. He talked often with his parents and seemed clear that mood-altering chemicals weren't for him. They supported his decision, but they also knew—and let him know—that in adolescence he might change his mind. They wanted him to know that if he did, the lines of communication would nevertheless still be open.

At 15 Randy still hadn't tried any mood-altering substances, but he was feeling curious. Several of his friends drank beer, and they didn't seem to have any problems. Actually, they seemed to have a good time laughing and telling jokes. All his life he had heard about all the terrible problems people had from drinking and using drugs. Maybe it wasn't such a big deal after all.

Randy mentioned this to Frank, who replied, "So, you're thinking of trying some alcohol?"

Randy said, "I don't know. I'm just curious, I guess. The other kids don't seem to have big problems."

His dad replied, "That may be, but everyone is different. It may not be the same for you, even though I hope it won't be a problem. I hope that if you do decide to try alcohol, we can talk about it."

"OK, but I haven't decided I will," Randy said.

Next Friday night, Randy went out with his buddies. One of them had brought a couple of six-packs along. This time when they offered Randy a beer, he took it. He noticed a strange feeling of apprehension, and then he felt warm and comfortable. He continued to drink.

The next thing he knew, he was at home and it was morning. He couldn't remember how he had gotten home or much of what had happened the previous evening. He was frightened. He called his friend and found out he seemed to have had a good time and had gotten a ride home. His friend was puzzled to hear that Randy couldn't remember.

Randy told his parents he wanted to talk with them. He told them what had happened. Emily began to cry. Frank said, "It sounds like you had a blackout. That's a sign that you're an alcoholic. It usually doesn't happen that fast but it can. What do you think?"

"That's what I was afraid of," Randy said. "It was just like you had described it to me, and it scared me. I guess I get to go to meetings for me now. I think that would be best. I don't want my life to have to fall apart for me before I learn. I've learned that from you guys." Emily hugged him, and Randy said, "It's all right, I always knew this could happen. You helped me be prepared for this."

Honest and open communication made a big difference with Randy. In the following story, Babs also experienced getting a lot of help from her mother because her mother was so open and nonjudgmental.

Dialogue with a 16-Year-Old Girl

Babs, a 16-year-old junior in high school, liked to go out on weekends. Her mother, Susan, had been in recovery for over a year. Although her mother worried about teen drug and alcohol use, Babs and Susan had worked on honest communication in recovery and had developed a good relationship, even though they didn't always see things the same.

Babs came home from school on Thursday and told her mother she'd been invited to a party that Friday night, and she wanted to go. "All the kids in my group are going," she said. Susan asked where the party was, and did Babs think there would be drinking going on? Babs told her mother which friend was having the party, hesitated for a moment, and answered, "Yes, some of the guys are getting a keg."

Susan told Babs she needed a little while to think about it and would give her an answer by dinner time. Susan's first thought was, "No, I don't want you to go and be around that." She thought about what might happen if she told Babs she couldn't go. They'd probably have a fight. She knew she could handle that, but if her daughter really wanted to go she might sneak out the window. Worse, the next time this came up Babs might lie to her. Maybe she'd tell her mother she was going to a girlfriend's and go to the party. Communication would be shut down. Susan could lose her ability to have input and lose her opportunity to have influence with her daughter. If she sneaked out and something happened

141

at the party, Babs might feel she couldn't call her mother for help. Susan thought about her daughter. She had faith in her ability to make good decisions but she also had concerns. As soon as they sat down at the dinner table, Babs asked if she could go. Susan shared, "It scares me to have you go."

"Oh, Mom," Babs began.

"Please let me finish. Things might get out of control. Some kids might drink too much and get sick or drive. I'm afraid you could get hurt or worse, you might get raped."

"Mom! Really!"

"Well, it scares me. It probably won't happen but I'll feel better if you know that at this age your hormones are out of whack and when you add some alcohol to that, guys who usually behave one way may behave another. What would you do if that happened?"

"Mom, you worry too much."

"Do you feel that you can handle being there?"

Babs paused. Then she said, "Yes, I can handle it."

"OK, I trust your judgment. I want you to know that if it feels unsafe at any time or if you've had enough and need a ride home, you can call and I'll pick you up." Babs got up and gave her mother a big hug.

Saturday morning, when Babs came down to breakfast, Susan asked her how the party went. Babs said, "It was OK. The guys got sick and spent most of the night throwing up while the girls took care of them."

"Oh, that doesn't sound like much fun!"

"It wasn't," Babs said. "I don't know why people think parties are such a big deal. I'd rather go to a movie."

There is no substitute for open, noncritical communication with teens. When you give teenagers the opportunity to live their lives and to learn from their experiences, they will give you the opportunity to be there for guidance and support.

Parents have more life experience and a broader perspective than teens. When you have the courage to share your fears, even though your kids might dismiss them, you have raised their awareness of the issues and let them know it's OK to talk about anything.

Dialogue with a 17-Year-Old Boy

Sometimes teens can hear one concern more clearly than others. Here's an example.

Mom: Alan, I notice that you've been gaining weight. I can guess how much drinking you've been doing by looking at your belly.

Alan: Is it that noticeable?

Mom: Alan, I know that how you look is really important to you. You dress real sharp, spend hours on your hair, lift weights, and look in the mirror every chance you get. If you continue to drink as much beer as you do, it isn't going to improve your appearance, and yes, the beer belly is noticeable.

Alan shrugged and walked away. Several months later Alan asked his mom if she noticed anything different. She replied that she noticed that Alan was doing less drinking.

"You mean, I don't have a beer belly anymore?" asked Alan.

"I mean, you hardly have a beer belly anymore, and I can tell you're working on correcting that. Good for you!"

Alan grinned and walked away whistling.

With teens sometimes we need to say certain things, not because our kids will go out and do what we say, but because they'll think about it and they need the information. We present them with another picture, and it sticks in their mind. When they're ready, they can hear our words and it makes a difference. The following conversation is from the heart and loaded with useful information that kids will probably remember when they need it.

Dad: I want to talk to you about something because I see you and a lot of your friends ruining your bodies and self-respect over alcohol.

Son: Are you going to start in about drinking again? We just like kicking back. There's nothing else to do anyway. You and Mom drink, so what's the big deal? I wouldn't have any fun at a dance or a party if I were the only straight person there.

Dad: I notice that a lot of your friends are becoming addicted to drugs, and that's not cool. I think sometimes you think when you're drunk that you're fun and clever and popular. Being around a drunk is really a drag after a while. I think you kids have a lot of insecurities and fears, and you use alcohol to hide them and mask them. All it does is take you away from the life you want to live. When you're using, you show no respect for yourself or other people in your life.

Son: Dad, everyone drinks. You're just being uptight.

Dad: I wish you loved yourself and your body enough to stop using and drinking and to work on getting a life together instead. Using chemicals as much as you and your friends do is extremely risky. You're building habits you may find hard to change. Also, you're developing a tolerance for chemicals. That's very dangerous. It seems like you never have a day without being under the influence. Many people whose lives have become unmanageable because of drugs started off just that way. They didn't sit down and say, "I think I'll become an alcoholic." They did what you are doing, and before they knew it, they destroyed friendships, family, morals, and self-respect. If I could make you stop, I would, but I know you're the one who has to decide that. I don't intend to pretend that what you are doing is OK. I hope you'll think about the things I'm saying and consider them.

Son: Well, I'm not going to stop partying. I think you worry too much. It's OK, Dad. Lighten up!

This father knows that what kids do today is not necessarily what they'll do tomorrow. He trusts the delayed reaction that often happens with this age group. As long as the father operates on the principles of mutual respect, he can trust that the lines of communication will stay open and that he can continue to have an influence with his son.

We hope that the guidelines and sample dialogues presented in this chapter will help ease your fears and give you tools for helping your kids learn about drugs and their uses and possible abuses through communication that is honest, informative, open, and nonjudgmental.

Understand the Belief Behind the Behavior

There were three children in the Fitzpatrick family, 10-year-old Dale, 9-year-old Joel, and 7-year-old Bud. Mr. Fitzpatrick was an alcoholic. When he was drunk, he was emotionally abusive to the boys. Sometimes he would tell them to get out of his sight. Other times he would criticize them, tell them they were "good for nothing," and complain about his fate for being burdened with children.

Dale decided (unconsciously), "Dad is wrong. I'll prove that I'm worthwhile. I'm going to make something of my life. I'll do well in school and in college and get a good job. Someday I'll have children, and I will never treat them like this."

Joel decided, "Dad is right. Since I'm not good for anything, why try? I'll just goof around in school and hang around with the stoners. I'll never get close to anyone who expects anything of me. Who needs the criticism? I'll be as bad as my dad thinks I am!"

Bud decided, "Dad is right. I need someone to take care of me. I can get my mom, Dale, and my teachers to feel sorry for me and help me. I don't have to do much for myself, because I can get other people to do things for me."

Separate Realities—Same Situation, Different Decisions

Family members who experience the same situation together often make decisions that are very different. When they compare memories of an event, it looks as if they experienced separate and totally different events. Some family members who were present at the event may not remember it at all. They all develop their selective perceptions (decisions and beliefs) through which they filter life experiences.

Dale became a high achiever. Joel became a criminal. Bud became a charming manipulator who eventually married a woman who was willing to support him when he lost job after job. Each of the boys made different decisions about the treatment they received from their father. They formed different beliefs about themselves, life, and others. Their behavior was directly related to their decisions and beliefs.

As we discussed in Chapter 1, what happens to people is never as important as the decisions and beliefs they create about what happens to them. Their behavior is then based on those decisions and beliefs. The decisions and beliefs people form are directly related to the primary goal of all people—the need to find belonging and significance.

The Primary Goal of All People

All people want to belong and feel significant. Dale decided he could find belonging and significance through achievement. Joel decided he couldn't belong in a useful way, but could find belonging and significance with his criminal friends. Bud decided he couldn't belong and find significance through his own efforts, but he could by getting others to take care of him.

The decisions children make about belonging and significance are infinite. The important thing to understand is that people are active participants (not victims) in the process of deciding things about themselves, others, and life; and their behavior is based on those decisions. Understanding the decision-making process and how children create their beliefs is the first step to understanding their behavior. With this understanding, you can be encouraging to your kids and provide opportunities for them to change unhealthy beliefs and behaviors.

The Influence of Birth Order: Family Constellation

In previous chapters, we have discussed how the family atmosphere and parenting styles influence children. There is no doubt that the effects of addiction in the family invite further discouragement. An important factor that is often overlooked is the influence of birth order. Children's first decisions about how they can belong are made in the context of their birth order.

Children are not consciously aware of the process, but they look around in their family and make comparisons with their siblings. These comparisons are called *competition*. They try to figure out how they can belong and

149

be significant in areas different from those they believe are already taken by their siblings. If one child is already good in academics, another child might try to be "popular," another "the good child," another "the rebel," another the "charming manipulator." It is important to remember we are talking about possibilities, not stereotypes.

The firstborn child in a family is the first child faced with finding his or her place of belonging. Often oldest children decide they belong by being "the first and the best." (Remember, this process is not conscious.) When another child arrives on the scene, they might decide they can be significant by being responsible, helpful, smart, perfectionistic, and the boss.

The second child usually decides the *first* place is taken and is faced with the challenge of choosing a different way to be special. The exceptions are those who decide to challenge the firstborn for the spot of being first and best, and become "Avis" kids who "try harder." Second-born children may choose to be easygoing, socially popular, noisier, or less responsible and adequate because of their perceived inability to keep up with their older sibling.

If a third child is born, the second child becomes a middle child and may feel squeezed, deciding "life is unfair," with neither the privileges of the oldest nor the advantages of the youngest.

Youngest children might decide to be cute and entertaining. Some decide they need to be taken care of and learn the skills of charm and manipulation. They often think they are *entitled* to special treatment. Others decide to become *speeders*—to do better than the rest.

Children who have no siblings (only children) often share the characteristics of the oldest or the youngest. It depends on what they decide. Some find belonging and significance by finding a way to be special or to be the "one and only."

These descriptions are based on research that shows *typical* decisions made by people of the same birth order. There are many exceptions, and each individual also makes many unique decisions. The whole point of discussing typical and unique decisions made by people is to help you become aware that your children are making decisions that affect their behavior. Understanding this process can help you become more sensitive and aware of separate realities and the possibility for change.

This information on birth order can offer hope to families in recovery who want to change but who feel tied to their past. Learning more about the decisions based on birth order can help relieve some guilt from the using parents, who blame themselves for all the problems their children have. Many of the kids' discouraging decisions did not have anything to do with the problems of chemical abuse in the family. Their beliefs about themselves were influenced by their competition with siblings for their place in the family.

Another model that can help you understand more about competition in the family has been provided by Sharon Wegsheider-Cruse in her book, *Another Chance* (Palo Alto, CA: Science & Behavior Books, 1981). She popularized four roles she calls "the hero," "the scapegoat," "the lost child," and "the mascot." These roles are stereotypes of decisions children make on how to find their special place in the family. These roles are often found in families with chemical dependency. They also appear in families where no one was abusing chemicals. The four roles provide a helpful way to understand more about the beliefs behind your children's behavior.

Often the hero will be the firstborn; the youngest, the mascot; and the lost child or the scapegoat, the second. These parallels are not hard and fast. Children can take on a combination of roles. Birth-order decisions are also altered when there are (1) gaps of four or more years between children, (2) blended families, and (3) same-sex children close in age.

Later, we present an activity called "The Family Pie" to help you identify how your children specifically see themselves in the family. For now, as you read the information on roles, you can make some guesses about how each of your children may have decided they can belong in your family and what their beliefs might be. Once you know what your children believe, you have an opportunity to help them explore other possibilities that work better to create a happier and healthier future.

The Hero

The hero is characteristically the child who is a high achiever. He or she has a lot of friends, may be good in sports and/or get good grades. Heroes seem to be successful at everything they do. They are under a lot of pressure to perform so they can provide the sense of worth for their family. They are concerned with doing what's right. These are the children who often take on the parenting role as their using parents are unavailable. One unconscious belief is that they might be inadequate no matter how hard they try. They feel very discouraged when no matter how hard they work or how many awards they win, they can't fix the problem at home.

Heroic children have underlying feelings of guilt, shame, and embarrassment. They often grow up to be workaholics who drive themselves relentlessly and take on responsibilities for those around them. They may marry someone who is chemically dependent (thus getting another chance to try to fix the problem) or may turn to chemical use themselves, in an attempt to relax and take some of the pressure off for a little while.

Kelly is a typical family hero. She is only 12 years old and has a 9-year-old sister and a 5-year-old brother. Her mother has had back problems for as long as she can remember and has taken prescription medication for the pain. She has become addicted to the medication and often displays the behaviors of an alcoholic.

When Kelly comes home from school, she never knows in what condition her mother will be. When her mother is pain-free and unmedicated, the children can get a snack, do chores, and play.

Other times Kelly comes home and finds her mother crying or screaming or asleep in a medicated stupor. Then Kelly sends the younger children to their room and is stuck with her mother for what seems like forever. She waits on her mother hand and foot while trying to calm her down. When her mother is asleep, Kelly runs into the kitchen to get dinner for the family and later gets the younger children ready for bed. Kelly is the family hero who has taken on the role of mother. She has assumed the adult responsibilities necessary to make the household function.

The Scapegoat

Scapegoats are children who have decided not to compete for the hero's place. They find belonging and significance by seeking negative attention. They appear to be sullen and defiant. Trouble seems to follow them everywhere. Their parents often get telephone calls from school complaining about their behavior or poor grades. Later they may have trouble with the law. They often look as though they don't care about what's happening. This is their way of covering the underlying feelings of anger, shame, guilt, and pain. One unconscious belief is that they're no good. As teenagers, they might become pregnant or become involved in chemicals (it's a way to numb the pain as well as rebel and be defiant) or have problems at work.

Larry is a typical scapegoat. He is three years older than his sister Lucy. When something happens to Lucy, Larry always seems to be at fault. He calls her "Miss Goodie Two-Shoes." It seems as if she can do no wrong and he can do no right. Larry's mom, Elaine, often complains about having a difficult time controlling Larry.

Elaine had been taking tranquilizers for years. She didn't see it as a problem even though she often took more than prescribed. Her excuse was that she took extras just to take the edge off her stress, because Larry was such a difficult child. One afternoon Larry was yelling at Lucy for not returning a cassette tape she had borrowed from him. He grabbed the tape out of her boom box, and Lucy yelled at him to get out of her room. Elaine came running up the stairs screaming at Larry, "Leave your sister alone! Get out of her room! What the *hell* do you think you're doing?"

Larry tried to explain, "But she took my tape and..."

Elaine interrupted, "I don't care. You're always picking on her. You're just rotten! Mrs. Johnson (Larry's teacher) called and said you cut school and haven't handed in your assignments this week."

Larry tried to defend himself, "She's out to get me in trouble. She's just a bitch!"

"Don't you use that kind of language!"

Elaine's husband arrived home from work and heard the yelling. He raced upstairs and yelled at Larry, "Get to your room!" He started shoving Larry into his room as he took off his belt. He started hitting Larry as the boy cowered in the corner of his room.

The Lost Child

Lost children are the quiet children, the loners. It's almost as though these children are invisible. They have learned to hold everything in and not make waves as a protection against the outbursts of their chemically dependent parent. They have few friends, tend to be withdrawn, and are good at creating their own fantasy world. They usually do average work in school and don't do anything that will draw attention to themselves. They provide some relief to the family because this is one child no one has to worry about, or more accurately, even think about. No one is aware of the child's needs and underlying feelings of loneliness, fear, sadness, and hurt.

One unconscious belief of these children is that they are unimportant. As adults, they might find themselves isolated socially, having little zest for life. They often have difficulty making decisions and create stress-related medical problems. Chemicals may offer some relief from the isolation and pain.

Seven-year-old Alice is a typical lost child. One day her father didn't come home after work. At about 7 P.M., her mother began calling the local bars, trying to locate him. She told Alice and her two older brothers that their father would be late, so they ate dinner without him. As soon as the father walked through the door, his wife began attacking him: "Where *were* you? I called your brother's house and his wife said the two of you went out for a few drinks. How much did you have to drink?"

Alice went into her room, the sound of swearing and abuse resounding throughout the house. She grabbed her doll and went into her closet. She shut the door and sat down on the floor, tears dripping on her doll. Then Alice heard her dad stomping down the hall, swearing and slamming doors loudly. She could hardly breathe, so she sat still and quiet until she fell asleep.

The Mascot

Mascots are cute, charming, funny, and amusing. Rarely are they listened to or taken seriously. They are energetic, on the go, and always "on." Their role in the family is to provide fun and humor and to keep things light and entertaining. They supply the comic relief covering the underlying feelings of fear, shame, and hurt. Mascots grow up needing to be taken care of, and often find a hero to provide that care. They appear irresponsible and often avoid tasks because they never learned the skills needed. One unconscious belief is that they're not capable.

Susie is a typical mascot. One day her father, Jim, called her mother, Karen, and invited her to join him near his office for a few drinks. Karen told Jenny, her oldest daughter, to give her three younger sisters dinner and to get them off to bed. After the children were in bed, they heard their mother and father come home fighting. Jim and Karen screamed abuses at each other and threw things. Finally it was quiet.

In the morning, Jenny got Susie (the youngest) up and helped her get dressed in her jumper with the pink bows. Jim had left for work already, and Karen was fixing breakfast. There was a rectangular hole in the wall where the bottom of a lamp might fit. Susie just smiled and asked her Mom to look at the dance she could do. When she was done, everyone clapped. Susie curtsied, and everyone laughed. Everyone was thus able to avoid the uncomfortable feelings they had about the terrible fight last night.

Later in this chapter, we will discuss methods that give each of these children opportunities to make new decisions. If you can see any of your children fitting these roles, you will be able to personalize the suggestions to your family. Do any of your children fit the description of hero, scapegoat, lost child, or mascot? "The Family Pie" activity, from the book, *To Know Me Is to Love Me* (Petaluma, CA: Practical Press, 1990), by Lynn Lott and Dru West is included here to help you identify roles being played in your family.

The Family Pie

The following example of a family pie describes the characteristics of children in a chemically dependent family, using the four roles to which we have been referring.

The Family Pie

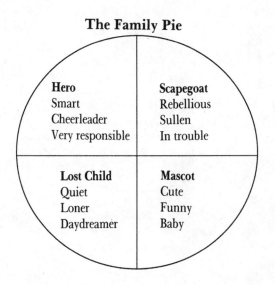

| **Hero**
Smart
Cheerleader
Very responsible | **Scapegoat**
Rebellious
Sullen
In trouble |
| **Lost Child**
Quiet
Loner
Daydreamer | **Mascot**
Cute
Funny
Baby |

To get more specific information as to how your children see themselves, divide the following circle into the number of slices corresponding to the number of children in your family. Write the name of each child in a slice along with at least three words to describe him or her. Notice if your children resemble the characteristics described by the hero, the scapegoat, the mascot, or the lost child. Do some of your children take on more than one role? Are your children unique but different from the roles we have described?

My Family Pie

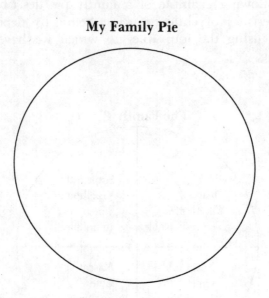

Children tend to think in black and white. They believe that the "Family Pie" has just so many pieces to go around. Therefore, if a piece is taken by one child, the other child decides to take another, very different piece. These unconscious decisions or beliefs remain with children into adulthood.

This information and understanding can help you encourage your children to make new decisions. Sometimes kids think they are loved only if they act according to the descriptions in the "Family Pie" activity. Kids will make dramatic changes automatically when you stop focusing on changing them and instead focus on helping them know that love and acceptance aren't conditional. Once you understand that the foundation of encouragement is unconditional love and acceptance, you can build on this foundation with specific approaches that help children who have assumed each role.

Encouraging the Hero

Children who have been heroes need validation that they were indeed helpful in a time of need. The family *was* a mess and needed their help. Their taking over and being helpful in many cases enabled the family to function when their parents weren't doing their job effectively. But now that time is over. In recovery, parents can help heroes learn to work together with the whole family. They are still needed as helpers, but not as caretakers. You don't want to take their role away from them or try to change them. What you *can* do is give them a chance to learn how to be helpful while creating more balance between giving and receiving in their lives.

Heroes can still be helpers by sharing their ideas at family meetings. They can learn to help younger siblings by doing *less* for them so the younger kids can learn to be *in*dependent and *inter*dependent instead of *de*pendent. They can be encouraged to express what they need and want. They can learn that they are OK when they make mistakes and aren't perfect.

Heroes feel less pressure to be perfect when parents model that it's OK to make a mistake by sharing their mistakes and what they learned from them. Parents can also take time to relax and to play, and to invite the hero to join them. This gives heroes an opportunity to experience some time that's not oriented toward achievement.

Remember our hero Kelly, who took care of her 9-year-old sister and 5-year-old brother while her mother slept, cried, or screamed under the influence of her drugs? One of the things Kelly did was to remind her younger siblings about their table manners and nag them about playing with their food. She didn't want her mother to start screaming one more time.

When Kelly's mother got into recovery, she began to notice Kelly's behavior at dinner. One day she called Kelly aside and told her, "You really love your brother and sister, don't you?" Kelly said she did, and Mom continued, "Would you like to help them grow up?" Kelly nodded. "If I showed you some ways in which what you're doing isn't helping, would you be willing to do something different that *would* help?" Kelly said she would.

Kelly's mom told her how nagging her brother and sister about food at the table was inviting them to believe they were incapable. She asked Kelly if she'd be willing to pretend to button her mouth and make no comments about her siblings' eating habits. If she forgot, Mom asked if she could signal Kelly with one finger on her lips.

Kelly agreed. At the next meal, much to the younger kids' surprise, Kelly said nothing. At the next family meeting, Kelly wanted to talk about her brother and sister's table manners. During the discussion, everyone agreed that they could all improve their manners. They decided they would have "manners night" on Thursday nights. On this night they would teach manners and use good manners. They laughed and learned as everyone exaggerated using excellent manners. Every other night,

Kelly allowed the other kids to be responsible for their eating habits, even when they made mistakes.

Notice how Kelly's mother took an active role to encourage Kelly and in doing so helped the whole family. Kelly experienced considerable relief knowing that she didn't have to take care of her mother and that her mother was there to parent the younger kids.

Encouraging the Scapegoat

We can encourage scapegoats by letting them know, in a firm and kind manner, instead of with humiliation and punishment, when their behavior is inappropriate. We can set limits and share clear explanations of what we will do and follow through with action. When we listen to them express their feelings, we can hear their anger and their hurt and let them know how appropriate it is for them to be feeling that way. Feelings are always appropriate. Actions are often inappropriate. We can work on building a friendship to help them heal the hurt. Being able to separate the person from the behavior is crucial; for example, "I love you and value who you are, and I don't like what you're doing right now."

Let's look at how Larry's mother, Elaine, learned to encourage him and help Larry get out of the role of scapegoat. Before Elaine got into recovery, Larry seemed angry and belligerent most of the time. Everyone thought he was the cause of most problems and arguments in the family. He was always blamed for starting trouble if his sister Lucy was upset.

For as long as Elaine could remember, Larry had had problems at school as well as at home. For years, she threatened and yelled in the mornings to get him up and off to school. She would remind and lecture him about his homework in the evenings. The results were continued poor grades, school conferences, notes home from his teachers, tension and fighting at home, and deterioration of the family relationships.

Elaine thought she was a failure as a mother, and Lucy was embarrassed by her brother's behavior. Elaine found a doctor who understood chemical dependency and helped her get off her prescription drugs. She advised her to get into an AA program where she began to work a program of recovery. Still feeling discouraged as a parent, she began reading *I'm on Your Side: Resolving Conflict with Your Teenage Son or Daughter* (Rocklin, CA: Prima, 1991), by Jane Nelsen and Lynn Lott. From reading this book, she could see she needed to help Larry by taking a totally different approach.

The next morning Larry didn't get out of bed when his alarm clock buzzed. Instead of screaming, Elaine sat down on Larry's bed and suggested he drop out of school. Larry could hardly believe what he was hearing and said, "Do what?"

Elaine repeated, "Why don't you drop out of school? You aren't going anyway, and I'm not going to fight with you over it anymore."

Larry told her he didn't want to drop out but that he'd like to go to the continuation school, because he was so far behind he thought he'd never catch up. Elaine told him she'd work with him to arrange that. Larry scheduled an appointment with his school counselor, and Elaine went with him to arrange for the transfer and help plan the courses.

That night Elaine told Larry that although she had wanted to help him in the past she recognized that yelling, nagging, and punishment weren't helpful. She told him that she wasn't going to get him up in the mornings or nag him about his schoolwork. She knew that he was capable of dealing with his schoolwork and had confidence that he would—one way or another. She said that for the first time she realized she had to accept this was his life, and if he made mistakes he could learn from them. She also told Larry that she'd like to spend some time with him. They agreed to go out for pizza the following evening.

Elaine decided that instead of turning their time together into an inquisition, this would be a good time to practice being curious and to really listen to Larry. She was ready to discover who he was, understand what he was feeling, what was important to him, and how he saw things. She was hopeful this could be a new beginning for them.

Larry did not talk at all during their pizza date. Elaine could feel that he didn't trust her to treat him respectfully. However, she stuck to her decision to treat him kindly and firmly when he misbehaved, to keep the lines of communication open, and to keep scheduling special time with Larry.

Larry missed a few days of school and didn't complete some of his assignments. Elaine resisted her temptation to interfere and respected Larry's ability to deal with the teacher directly. The teacher told him it would just take him longer to finish the course and receive credit. When Larry finally understood that it was up to him, he did very well. He finished several courses in the continuation school and went back to the regular high school the next fall.

As they continued their pizza dates, Larry started talking with Elaine; not as much as she would like, but significantly more than in the past. Instead of badgering him to talk more, she felt grateful for the progress and kept listening with curiosity. She also started sharing her thoughts and feelings with him.

When Larry and Lucy got into fights, Elaine now "put them in the same boat"—that is, treated them the same instead of taking sides. She told them at a family meeting that she would do this. Sometimes she told them to go outside or to another room if they wanted to fight. Other times she went to her own room and read a book until they stopped fighting. If they came to her room and tried to get her involved, she would say, "Excuse me. I'm getting into the shower now." And she did.

Parents typically try to identify a culprit in a sibling fight. The culprit is usually the same child over and over. This is one way to create a scapegoat and help him or her keep this role. Not identifying a culprit helps the child get out of the scapegoat role.

Elaine's methods were effective. Larry remained a little defiant, but Elaine didn't get hooked very often. He accepted more responsibility for his behavior and was more cooperative in family meetings. The whole family enjoyed the improved closeness.

Encouraging the Lost Child

Lost children need contact on a one-to-one basis. It's important to reach out to build a relationship with these children, who have been hiding their needs as a way of being safe. Small starting steps that involve touch, such as holding hands, a kiss on the cheek, and spontaneous hugs, are important ways of making a connection. Parents need to point out and encourage their strengths, talents, and creativity. Parents also need to help these children by inviting them to be important parts of the family.

Seven-year-old Alice, the child who hid in the closet when her mother and father fought, needed a lot of encouragement. Her parents were aware of how quiet she was. When they were using alcohol, that quietness was a relief to them. They weren't called to school for problems, and they didn't have to show up for an awards assembly or a play, as they did for their two boys. Alice required very little attention. She just stayed out of the way.

As Alice's father, Dick, learned about the role of the lost child, he wanted to reach out to Alice. He set up family meetings once a week and posted an agenda on the refrigerator so the entire family could meet together to share and problem solve. At first Alice was reluctant to participate. Dick told Alice that he understood it was scary for her to have the family meet together but that he wanted her to attend anyway because the family really needed her ideas. Dick made a point of asking Alice for her ideas or how she felt about different things that were brought up.

With her dad's encouragement, Alice began to bring up the things that were bothering her. Because there was no evaluating or criticizing during the brainstorming part of problem solving, Alice began to share her ideas. At one meeting, Dick shared that he wanted the family to have more fun together, as a family. Everyone shared their ideas for having fun. Alice shared that she thought it would be fun to play miniature golf. It was Dick's turn to choose from one of the suggestions. When he chose miniature golf, he noticed that Alice sat up a little taller in her seat.

Dick also made a point of tucking Alice into bed each night, and they began a game of sharing one feeling each had felt that day. They ended the game with a hug. Dick was pleased at how little effort it took to help Alice stop acting like a lost child.

Encouraging the Mascot

It's crucial to begin taking mascots seriously, so that they learn they can develop skills other than being cute and entertaining. Parents can ask them for their ideas and encourage them to share their feelings. You can give them the opportunity to grow up and to be responsible by having them share in the chores, get themselves up in the morning with an alarm clock, choose their own clothes, make their lunch, and manage their allowance. They also need lots of affection.

Jim and Karen spent much of their married life drinking and using together. When Karen went into treatment, Jim decided it was time to stop his drinking and drugging as well. With the help of AA and NA, the couple made many changes in their lives.

Jim and Karen realized how much they babied their youngest daughter, Susie, and how discouraged she had become. They asked Susie if she would like the opportunity to be more grown up. At first she wasn't sure what they meant, but as her parents described all the things they knew she could do, Susie was intrigued with the idea.

The family set up a system for doing chores at dinner time. Susie decided she wanted to set the table each night. Karen and Jim asked the older children, and especially big sister Jenny, to help by *not* jumping in and setting the table for Susie. They agreed. Each night, whoever cooked announced dinner, and Susie got the silverware and dishes and set the table.

One night Susie was watching TV when dinner was announced. When she looked up ten minutes later, she saw everyone sitting at the table waiting. Susie jumped up and got the table set. The food was served without a word said about waiting.

Karen showed Susie how to use the washing machine, and when she was almost out of underwear she would do her own laundry. She even did her older brother's laundry once to help him out. Susie began making her own lunches and stopped complaining to her mom about what she had to eat. With these opportunities, Susie's confidence in herself became more apparent.

When you understand your children's thinking, the beliefs they have about themselves, others, and life, you are in a better position to influence them in positive ways. Information about the family constellation and roles enables you to look at your children's behavior and understand the beliefs behind their behavior. This information will give you many clues about what your children need to have the opportunity to change some of their decisions and beliefs that are not helpful to them. You are much more effective when you deal with the belief behind the behavior, instead of only with the behavior.

Chapter

10

Redirect Misbehavior with Encouragement

When parents are faced with a misbehaving child, it's hard to remember there is a belief behind every behavior. When a child is misbehaving, parents usually get hooked. At the moment, they could care less about the belief— all they want to do is stop the obnoxious behavior. Many parents get hooked into more than just wanting to stop the behavior—they want to punish, win, get even, or give up. This is called *discouragement*. The basis of misbehavior, both parents' and their children's, is discouragement.

Children misbehave when *they* believe they don't have belonging and significance. It doesn't matter if *others* think they belong and are significant. What matters is what *they* believe—their behavior is based on what they believe. Alfred Adler and Rudolph Dreikurs discovered this many years ago. Adler called it "private logic." Dreikurs often said, "A misbehaving child is a discouraged child who lacks a sense of belonging and significance."

Parents become discouraged when they witness the misbehavior of their children. They may believe they are inadequate, powerless, or incapable of making children do what they are *supposed* to do.

Rudolf Dreikurs studied hundreds of children and discovered four mistaken goals of misbehavior based on four mistaken beliefs. He called them "mistaken goals" and "mistaken beliefs" because children (and adults) often come to mistaken conclusions about how to find belonging and significance. These mistaken conclusions take them to the "useless, nonproductive" side of life instead of to the "useful, productive" side of life.

Four Mistaken Goals of Misbehavior

Understanding the four mistaken goals of misbehavior can give you information you can use to help your children feel better about themselves, change their decisions, and behave in more acceptable ways. You can use this information to encourage your kids.

Undue Attention as a Goal

The first goal of misbehavior is called "undue attention." Children who seek this mistaken goal believe they are important only when they keep others busy with them. They are skilled at getting people to notice them and give them special service.

Everyone wants attention. The mistake in the goal of undue attention is the belief that "I'm not significant unless I have almost constant attention." The misbehavior occurs when children seek attention incessantly or at inappropriate times.

Diagnostic Clues There are two clues you can use to help you understand which of the four mistaken goals is the basis of your children's misbehavior. The first clue is what you *feel* when you get involved in the behavior. If you listen to your feelings, they will help you understand the goal of your children's misbehavior or the belief behind the behavior. The second clue is what the child *does* when you try to correct the behavior in inappropriate ways.

When the mistaken goal is undue attention, parents feel *annoyed, worried,* or *irritated.* When you react by getting involved with such children and by giving them the attention they want, they temporarily stop misbehaving. Soon after you stop giving them attention, and especially if you give your attention to someone else, they start demanding your attention again. When you give children undue attention, you are unknowingly reinforcing their mistaken belief that they're OK only when others are busy with them.

Here is an example. Cindy was on the telephone with her sponsor. Her 5-year-old daughter, Sandy, stopped coloring with her crayons and asked her mom for a glass of juice. Cindy replied, "I'm on the phone, you'll have to wait."

In less than a minute, Sandy picked up her doll and came over to Cindy. She looked up and asked sweetly, "Now can I have some juice?"

Cindy looked down and said, "Not now, honey, I'm busy."

Sandy sat down on the floor and within minutes began tugging on the telephone cord. Cindy interrupted her conversation and said, "You're bugging me, go play at your table." Sandy got up, walked over to her crayons, and started to draw.

When Cindy hung up the phone, she was feeling irritated with her daughter. She scolded, "Why can't you leave me alone when I'm on the phone?" Then she felt worried and guilty, and sat down to color with Sandy to make up for neglecting her to talk on the phone. Cindy didn't notice Sandy's smile of satisfaction.

Cindy's feelings of irritation, worry, and guilt could help her understand that her daughter was feeling discouraged and believed she's important only when her mother is noticing her and giving her special service. Cindy could help Sandy by focusing on the needs of the situation and respecting herself and Sandy.

The needs of the situation are defined by what is appropriate. It is appropriate for Cindy to have time to herself and to have an opportunity to talk on the phone. It is appropriate for Sandy to have periods of time when she is getting attention and times when she can entertain herself. Cindy can show respect for herself and Sandy when she allows herself appropriate self-time and finds respectful ways to teach Sandy that she has belonging and significance without undue attention.

Cindy learned about the four goals of mistaken behavior and could see that Sandy's misbehavior was based on the mistaken goal of undue attention. She came up with a plan.

Encouraging Children Who Have the Mistaken Goal of Undue Attention

Cindy called her sponsor and asked for her help. She explained her plan to help Sandy learn that she could handle being on her own and entertain herself while Cindy was talking on the phone. (It's important to note that Cindy wasn't spending an unreasonable amount of time on the phone, wasn't being disrespectful to Sandy.)

The next day Cindy was checking in with her sponsor, and Sandy again interrupted her. This time Cindy continued to talk. Sandy continued to interrupt, but Cindy went on talking with her sponsor and gently put her hand on her daughter's shoulder. Sandy looked surprised, but tried again by asking her mother a question. Cindy continued talking to her sponsor. A few moments later, Sandy went off to entertain herself with her dolls.

Cindy respectfully ignored Sandy's bid for attention and stayed focused on her conversation. (She had warned her sponsor that she might not make sense during this training period because she knew she would be distracted by the interruptions, even though she wanted to practice not getting hooked by them.) Cindy used touch to nonverbally tell Sandy that she was loved and that her mother was busy. "I love you and I'm not available right now" conveys the message that the parent has confidence that the child is capable of taking care of herself for periods of time. It conveys the message that she can handle not being the center of attention and that cooperating with others is important. It invites the child to believe that "I am capable of managing myself."

Many parents created bad habits while they were using, and gave their kids undue attention. They tried to make up for periods of neglect by giving special service. Now they have an opportunity to create new habits by learning ways to give attention that encourage their kids.

We repeat, children *do* need attention. Attention helps them know they belong, they matter, they are loved, and others care about them. When they feel belonging and significance, they can develop the ability to care for others and to form loving relationships. When training children to stop demanding undue attention, it is important to schedule and spend special time with them so they experience appropriate attention.

Encouraging by Giving Special Time An effective way to give appropriate attention is through special time. This

173

is a time that is set up in advance, is limited, and happens on a regular basis. Both the parent and child can plan what they'll do together and when they'll do it.

Cindy decided to spend special time with Sandy every afternoon for fifteen minutes. She got Sandy involved in the planning. She asked Sandy whether 3:00–3:15 or 3:15–3:30 would be better for her, and Sandy chose 3:00–3:15. They agreed to play games, play with dolls, color, or read a story during that time. The next day, during their special time together, the telephone rang. Cindy let the answering machine take a message. She was following through on her word and letting Sandy know that their special time was too important for interruptions.

Some parents find that ten minutes to half an hour at bedtime is a good way to spend special time. When parents give their undivided attention to their children, by reading a story or talking or snuggling, they finish the day with focused quality time that is reassuring and calming to children. This can become part of the daily routine.

Younger children, aged 2 to 5, need short but frequent special time (five minutes several times a day). As children get older, the special time can be longer but less frequent (fifteen to twenty minutes once a day for 6- to 8-year-olds). Half an hour twice a week seems sufficient for most 9- to 12-year-olds. By the time kids become teenagers, parents are lucky to get a commitment from kids to spend special time with them once or twice a month.

Parents often get scared or discouraged because they have the picture that special time means expensive or elaborate child-dominated time. One way to eliminate this is to plan together and decide on amounts of time and things to do agreed on by both. Another solution is to make sure that you are 100 percent present during special time. One father found that all he had to do was come home from work, put down his belongings, and lie on the living room floor while the kids tackled him and wrestled with him. Small pieces of regular and consistent quality time are a wonderful way to mend broken bonds, establish nurturing and caring in relationships, and build trust.

Power as a Goal

The second mistaken goal of misbehavior is power. Children who seek this mistaken goal believe, "I'm important if I'm the boss. No one can tell me what to do." They are skilled at defeating the demands of adults. Sometimes they will be up front and say, "You can't make me!" Other times they may agree to demands and then simply not keep their agreements. Another way of showing that parents can't make them do what parents want is to agree to demands but do it below standard or slower than parents would like.

Everyone wants power. The mistake in the mistaken goal of power is the belief that "I'm not significant unless I defeat adults who want to control me." The misbehavior occurs when children seek power at the expense of their own welfare and at the expense of loving relationships. However, we have never seen a power-drunk child without a power-drunk adult close by. It takes two to engage in a power struggle.

When the mistaken goal of children is power, parents feel *angry, challenged,* or *threatened.* Most adults don't like to admit that they feel their power is being threatened. They excuse their need to use power and control by saying it is for the child's benefit, or that it is their job as a parent. These parents ignore that their discipline isn't working and that the child is not benefiting from their controlling methods.

When you react by getting involved in the power struggle with arguments, punishment, and threats, children feel obliged to intensify their play for power. It becomes a win-or-lose situation. Kids see their only choices as winning or losing. When you engage in the power struggle, you are unknowingly reinforcing their mistaken belief that they're OK only when they don't let others control them. If Cindy hadn't dealt with Sandy's undue attention, the conflict might have escalated to a power struggle as in the following scene.

Cindy is talking to her sponsor, and Sandy asks for a glass of juice. Cindy tells her to go play. Sandy stands next to her mother and screams, "I want a glass of juice now!"

Cindy yells back, "I'm on the phone; leave me alone!"

Sandy begins to cry and yells, "I want it now, I want it now!!"

Cindy screams back, "Get out of here!"

When Cindy hangs up, she is feeling angry and wants to make her daughter behave.

Cindy's angry feeling can help her understand that her daughter is discouraged and mistakenly believes that she is important if she is in charge. Cindy's natural response, wanting to prove to Sandy that she is the mother and that she is in charge, only reinforces Sandy's mistaken belief that her only choice is to win or lose.

Encouraging Children Who Have the Mistaken Goal of Power Parents need to get out of the power struggle and to use methods based on maintaining dignity and respect for parent and child. If Cindy respects herself and Sandy, she won't fight and she won't give in. Giving in to the demands of our children only intensifies their need for power.

Another way to give children a sense of positive power is to provide an opportunity for them to make choices.

When people are powerless over the use of chemicals, their choices are limited and it is impossible to focus on empowering others with choices. Since Cindy has stopped using chemicals, she has more choices and can empower her daughter through choices.

Empowering by Giving Choices As a parent it is your responsibility to set the parameters or the limits and to give your children the freedom to choose within the safety of those limits. This encourages children to feel both empowered and safe.

Cindy can give her daughter the choice of remaining in the room and behaving, or going into her room if she wants to throw a temper tantrum. There's no judgment of her daughter's behavior, and there's no fighting about it. Cindy can redirect Sandy to a more appropriate place for a temper tantrum, her room. Sometimes this works, and sometimes power-drunk children refuse to go to their rooms. Dreikurs encouraged parents to avoid power struggles by deciding what *they* will do instead of what they will try making *their children* do. Cindy can withdraw from the power struggle by deciding what *she* will do, by going into her bedroom to continue her conversation on the extension telephone.

Cindy began to think in terms of other choices she could offer Sandy. Cindy would put out two sets of clothes for the following day, and ask Sandy which outfit she wanted to wear. Sandy really enjoyed choosing and was pleased with herself. Breakfast went the same way. Cindy would say, "I'm making eggs for breakfast. Would you like scrambled or soft-boiled eggs?" If Sandy asked for pancakes, Cindy would reply that wasn't one of the choices for today and repeat the options. Because Sandy had the freedom to choose, she was cooperative and picked from what was available or did without.

Encouraging by Empowering It is important to help our children feel empowered so they can appreciate their abilities and have a sense of competence and capability. They need to have some control and power in their lives. When we feel empowered, we use power appropriately and productively.

For example, Cindy can empower Sandy by providing an appropriate-size container that's easily accessible and by teaching Sandy how to pour her own juice. She can go through the steps to train her daughter by giving her many tools and skills to feel capable and competent. And Sandy can use her power to help solve problems during family meetings.

Empowering by Holding Family Meetings Family meetings (as discussed in Chapter 7) are extremely effective for children whose misbehavior is based on the mistaken goal of power. "I need your help" is one of the most inviting and encouraging statements you can make to these children. In fact, family meetings can be encouraging to children in any of the four mistaken goals of misbehavior. In family meetings, children can use their power to help solve problems, make suggestions, and have a voice in how they would like things to go in their family. They also have a chance to express their feelings.

Revenge as a Goal

The third mistaken goal of misbehavior is called revenge. These children feel hurt by others and believe they have the right to seek justice. They can be very skilled at striking out and hurting back. Sometimes they feel hurt by the circumstances of their lives and take it out on anyone who comes into their world. Children raised in families plagued by chemical dependency often get even by hurting their teachers or counselors who try

178

to help them. Too many get even by hurting themselves through drug abuse, dropping out of school, or suicide. Some try to hurt their parents by not accomplishing the things their parents want.

It is a normal reaction to want to hurt someone who has hurt you. The mistake in the goal of revenge is the belief that "I don't belong, but at least I can be significant by hurting back."

When the mistaken goal of children is revenge, parents feel *shocked, hurt,* or *disgusted.* Most adults don't like to admit that they feel hurt by their children's behavior. Instead, they too hurt back (sometimes unconsciously) by dealing out blame, shame, humiliation, and punishment. This creates a "revenge cycle."

When parents react by getting involved in the revenge cycle by dealing out blame and shame, they unknowingly reinforce the mistaken belief of their children that they don't belong but can at least hurt back. They don't learn how to belong in positive ways, so they continue their destructive behaviors. If Cindy hadn't resolved the power struggle with Sandy, the situation could have escalated to revenge as follows.

Cindy is talking to her sponsor, and Sandy comes over and says, "I want a drink. Give me some juice."

Cindy tells her to go play now. Sandy yells, "I want juice, now!"

Cindy shrieks back, "Not now, I'm on the phone, you'll have to wait."

Sandy yanks hard on the telephone cord, and the receiver bangs into Cindy's lip. "Ouch, you rotten kid, that hurt." Cindy reaches over and smacks Sandy's hand.

Sandy cries out, "I hate you!"

"How dare you say that? You're going to stay in your room and think about what a bad girl you've been!" Cindy drags Sandy to her room and leaves her there crying.

Cindy's shocked and hurt feelings are a signal that she is dealing with revenge. Sandy mistakenly believes her mother doesn't care about her. This hurts, so she wants to get even. Cindy's human reaction of overpowering her daughter by name calling, hitting, labeling her daughter "a bad girl," and banishing her to be alone in her room escalates the situation and fortifies Sandy's mistaken belief.

Encouraging Children Who Have the Mistaken Goal of Revenge To deal with this situation respectfully, Cindy could let Sandy know, without hurting Sandy back, that she hurt her when she pulled on the telephone cord. Again, she could give Sandy the choice of staying in the room and handling it or going to her room if she wants to have a tantrum. Cindy could finish her conversation and then sit down with Sandy and talk about what happened. She could ask Sandy if she'd like to get an ice cube and hold it on her lip, so Sandy could participate in making amends. Cindy could ask her daughter what she was upset or hurt about, and could listen to her feelings. Maybe other issues in their relationship need to be addressed. Cindy could also build a base of friendship by planning special times together.

Cindy could focus on Sandy's positive traits. When you are upset with your children, it's easy to lose perspective and just see how obnoxious they are. It takes work to remember that your children are lovable. The problem you have to deal with is their behavior, which is a reflection of their discouragement.

It doesn't work to make children feel worse through punishment so they'll behave better. Children *do* better when they *feel* better. Because the purpose of their misbehavior is to gain belonging and significance in some discouraged way, encouragement is the key to helping them change their misbehavior.

Encouraging by Focusing on Positive Characteristics
Parents find that identifying three positive characteristics in their children each day helps them keep a positive attitude about their children. A good time to mention these positive characteristics is at the beginning of family meetings. Hearing these compliments helps children believe they belong and have significance. They also experience belonging and significance when they participate in giving compliments, sharing feelings, and problem solving in family meetings.

Giving Up as a Goal

The fourth goal of misbehavior is giving up (assuming some disability). Children who give up are very discouraged and believe they are incapable. They want others to leave them alone and not expect anything from them.

Everyone wants to give up sometimes. The mistake in the goal of giving up is the belief that "I'm not significant. I don't have any skills. It's not possible for me to belong. I give up." Such children don't "misbehave" in the typical sense: their "misbehavior" is trying to get others to leave them alone.

When the mistaken goal of children is giving up, parents feel *despair, helplessness,* and *guilt.* Parents often take it personally and feel it is their fault when their children give up. These children are so skilled at getting people to believe they are incapable that parents feel helpless to help them. Parents often react to their children's display of helplessness by rescuing them and doing too much for them. This only confirms their belief that they can't do anything, so why try?

If Sandy's mistaken goal was giving up, the phone situation might look like the following: Cindy is on the telephone talking to her sponsor, and Sandy is sitting on the floor nearby. Cindy walks over to Sandy's little table and says, "Why don't you color a pretty picture while I'm on the telephone?" Sandy just looks down at her shoes. Cindy picks up the red crayon and says, "This is such a pretty color. Here, I'll start and make a flower. Come on, you can make the people." Sandy just shakes her head. Cindy replies in a frustrated tone, "Never mind, I can't get you to do anything. I give up!" She turns her back to Sandy and starts her telephone conversation. Sandy remains where she is, staring at the floor.

When Cindy hangs up, she feels helpless and discouraged. She doesn't know how to help Sandy feel capable. Cindy's helpless feeling is a signal that her daughter is deeply discouraged and believes she can't do anything right, so why do anything at all.

Encouraging Children Who Have the Mistaken Goal of Giving Up Cindy can stop feeling so discouraged herself and arrange opportunities for Sandy to discover that she has many abilities. For example, Cindy could put out two pairs of pants and two shirts and let Sandy pick the shirt and pants she wants to wear. "You really know how to put colors together" is an encouraging statement that acknowledges Sandy's success. When Sandy dresses herself, even though she may be mismatched, Sandy can encourage her by acknowledging what she did do: "You got yourself dressed!"

Encouraging by Allowing Contribution When Cindy is making the dinner salad, she can invite Sandy to participate in a small step, such as adding the cut cucumbers or carrots or putting out the salad bowls. Cindy can also let Sandy know that she has faith in her abilities: "I know you can do that." When Sandy says she can't, Cindy can persist in giving Sandy a job that is so simple she can't fail. It is important that Cindy be patient and gentle in the process. (Imagine trying to do all this while under the influence!) With patient encouragement, Sandy will experience that she is capable. Her contributions can keep getting more difficult as she experiences success.

"Mistaken Goal" Chart

The "mistaken goal" chart on page 186 at the end of the chapter offers a summary of the four "mistaken goals" of misbehavior, including the child's belief, the parents' feeling that is the first clue to understanding the belief behind the misbehavior, and a few hints on how to encourage the child.

For two chapters we have discussed the importance of understanding the belief behind a child's behavior. You cannot assume you know what your children are deciding and believing. You can use your feelings to give you a clue. You can also ask questions to check out their perceptions.

Asking Questions to Discover How Kids Think About Themselves

Adam wet his bed from the time he was 3 until he was 13. His family tried many different methods to deal with this problem. None of them worked.

No one wanted to go in Adam's room or sit near him. They said he smelled funny. One day in therapy, the therapist asked Adam if he could be any animal he wanted, what would he be and why? Adam said, "I'd like to be a puppy so everyone would hold me, pet me, and cuddle me."

Adam's mother took the cue and decided to sit with her arm around Adam every day. One day while they were sitting this way on the couch, Adam asked his mom, "Do you love me?"

"Of course I do, honey. Why do you ask?"

"Do you remember when I was a little kid, and one of the neighbor kids tried to trick me and get me to drink ant poison?"

"I sure do. Your sister hit the container out of his hand before you touched it. It was a good thing she was with you that day."

"Yeah, but that kid never got in any trouble for trying to kill me." At that point, Adam began to cry.

"Honey, of course he got in trouble. Dad and I went over and talked to his parents about what happened and told them he was not allowed to play in our yard anymore. As I remember, he got in a lot of trouble. Why are you crying?"

"Because I didn't think you cared if he killed me," said Adam.

"You didn't think we loved you, did you? I'm so sorry! Do you know now that Daddy and I love you very much?"

"Yes, Mom, and I'm glad that kid got in trouble."

It was no surprise that Adam's bed-wetting diminished and finally stopped. Up until asking him the animal question, no one ever knew how upset he was and about what.

Other questions can give a lot of information about how our kids think, including the following:

- What is your favorite story (or TV show) and why? Who do you like best in the story and why?

- If someone was writing a story about you for the newspaper, what would you want him or her to say?
- When Mommy (or Daddy) was drinking, what did you think or decide?

You can also ask your kids what they remember from when they were little and what they decided when it happened. It is important that you use this information to encourage and show love to your kids and never to humiliate or tease them.

Encouragement is the key to helping children believe they belong and feel significant. When they feel belonging and significance, their behavior will be productive and contributing. This does not mean they will be perfect and never misbehave. Life offers challenge after challenge as people learn and grow. When you understand your children's beliefs, you can help them learn and grow.

Mistaken Goal Chart

If the Parent/ Teacher Feels	And Tends to React by	And if the Child's Response Is	The Child's Goal Is	The Belief Behind the Child's Behavior Is	A Parent's/Teacher's Alternatives Include
Annoyed Irritated Worried	Reminding Coaxing	Stops temporarily, but later resumes same or another disturbing behavior	Undue attention (to keep others busy with him or her)	I count (belong) only when I'm being noticed or getting special service. I'm only important when I'm keeping you busy with me.	"I love you and _____." (example: I love you and not now). Give positive attention at other times. Avoid special service. Say it only once, then act. Plan special time. Set up routines. Take time for training. Use natural and logical consequences. Encourage. Redirect. Use family or class meetings. Touch without words. Ignore. Set up nonverbal signals.
Angry Provoked Challenged Threatened Defeated	Fighting Giving in Thinking: "You can't get away with it" or "I'll make you." Wanting to be right	Intensifies behavior Defiant compliance Feels he's won when parents are upset	Power (to be boss)	I belong only when I'm boss or in control, or proving no one can boss me. "You can't make me."	Ask for help. Don't fight and don't give in. Withdraw from conflict. Do the unexpected. Be firm and kind. Act, don't talk. Decide what you will do. Let routines be the boss. Leave and calm down. Develop mutual respect. Give limited choices. Set reasonable and few limits. Encourage. Redirect to positive power. Use family or class meetings.
Hurt Disappointed Disbelieving Disgusted	Retaliating Getting even Thinking: "How could you do this to me?"	Retaliates Intensifies Escalates the same behavior or chooses another weapon	Revenge (to get even)	I belong only by hurting others as I feel hurt. I can't be liked or loved.	Deal with the hurt feelings. Avoid feeling hurt. Avoid punishment and retaliation. Build trust. Use reflective listening. Share your feelings. Make amends. Show you care. Act, don't talk. Encourage strengths. Put kids in same boat. Use family or class meetings.
Despair Hopeless Helpless	Giving up Doing for Overhelping	Retreats further Passive No improvement No response	Giving up and being left alone	I belong only by convincing others not to expect anything of me. I am helpless and unable; it's no use trying.	Show faith. Take small steps. Stop all criticism. Encourage any positive attempt, no matter how small. Focus on assets. Don't pity. Don't give up. Set up opportunities for success. Teach skills and show how. Step back. Enjoy the child. Build on interests. Encourage, encourage, encourage. Use family or class meetings.

Source: Compiled by Barbara Mendenhall, M.A.

Nurture the
Child Within

Until she was 6 years old, Jill thought she was just about the cutest thing that ever lived. And then it happened. She was standing in front of the mirror next to her older sister, Mary. Mary looked at herself in the mirror and saw a pimple. In total disgust, she said to her reflection, "Oh, Mary, you are so ugly!" Jill wanted to make her sister feel better and said, "No, you aren't!" Mary retorted "Yes, I am, and you're just as ugly!"

Jill felt crushed. She was sure her sister knew more than she did. If her sister said she was ugly, she must be ugly. At that moment she made an unconscious decision that she was ugly. Jill spent many years of her life believing she was ugly. It didn't matter that many other people told her she was attractive—some even said beautiful. She believed what she had decided when she was 6 years old—that she was ugly.

When she was 16, a local business asked Jill to represent them in a beauty contest. During the contest, Jill excelled in the group segments, where she laughed and talked with the judges from a distance. But when it came time for her individual appearance before the judges, where she had to get closer, she refused to smile or talk with them. She was afraid they would notice how "ugly" she was. One of the judges asked, "Don't you ever smile?" Jill said, "No." She knew it was a stupid thing to say, but because she believed she was "ugly" she acted "ugly." Later she was told that she had come in fifth and probably would have won if she showed more personality during her individual time with the judges.

As a teenager, Jill overcompensated for her "ugliness" by trying to be very "good." She loved being the only one in her crowd who didn't swear, drink, or smoke. She could also climb higher and jump farther than any boy in the neighborhood. Her behavior was very competitive. Whenever she wasn't the best, Jill thought she was a failure. If she didn't believe she could be the best, Jill didn't try at all and missed out on many things she really wanted to do. Jill's actions were based on her unconscious beliefs and the feelings they generated.

Like Jill, most people came to conclusions as children that made sense at the time and may even have helped them survive. People carry along these unresolved issues from childhood complete with feelings, thoughts, and actions. The unconscious beliefs formed as children thus guide adult lives. Most people are not aware that the decisions made as children often create dysfunction and discouragement for them as adults. They may be clinging to beliefs that no longer fit current situations.

Most people have no idea what those beliefs are or even that they made those beliefs. Any current experience that unconsciously reminds them of their childhood experiences can trigger the old feelings and decisions. Without realizing, they use the same logic from their childhood to deal with current situations, whether it fits or not. What happens to people is never as important as the decisions they make. Their decisions motivate their behavior.

Many people go through their entire lives without realizing how much they can change their lives by getting in touch with their unconscious childhood beliefs. Once they become aware of the decisions they made as children, they can begin a healing process. When people discover what is going on in their thoughts, they can nurture "the child within" using the wisdom and skills available to them as adults. The process of discovery helps them review those decisions and choose other ways of thinking, feeling, and acting that may be more appropriate to their present situations.

Discovery

Recovering and understanding old decisions from the past is a process we call *discovery*. Discovery allows people to get in touch with their child within and learn more about what that child is unconsciously thinking, feeling, and encouraging them to do. Discovery gives you a chance to see that what is happening unconsciously on the inside may be influencing your behavior more than what is obvious from the outside.

One of the best ways to accomplish "discovery" is to remember scenes from your childhood to help you get reacquainted with the child within. We call these scenes *early memories*. When you describe an early memory, it helps to write the memory down. You may not remember your exact age at the time, but you can write down the age you think you might have been then. After you write out the memory, you can read it aloud and then underline the most vivid part. You also need to write down one or two words to describe the feelings you were experiencing as a child in this memory. Next you can ask yourself, "What did I decide at that time?" Often your childhood decision will be quite clear. At other times you may have to guess, because the decision was unconscious.

The child you discover in your early memories is called your child within. After you discover this "hidden" child, you can go back in your imagination and redo scenes from your past to heal the child within. By pretending you have a magic wand, you can rewrite the scene any way you want. When you rewrite the memory, you can experience different feelings and different decisions. This healing process helps you make better decisions in your current life. It soothes the pain from the past and helps you explore other options that may be more appropriate for you to use in your adult life.

Discovering the Child Within

Ann provides an example of the positive that can happen from discovering the child within. She recently started college after years of staying home with the kids. Ann came home from her first day at college excited to share her experiences with her family. When she walked into the house, a depressed feeling came over her. A trail of clothes and books led to the kitchen, where dirty dishes and food lay everywhere. From the other room came the blaring sound of the TV set. When Ann walked in to see what was happening, she saw her husband David slumped on the couch sound asleep under a pile of newspapers. The kids were nowhere to be found.

Ann started looking for the kids to get some help. When she found them, they said it wasn't fair that they should have to clean up because it was Dad's night to do the dishes, and they couldn't help it if he fell asleep. They started complaining about how Dad had been yelling and criticizing them. Ann felt torn, angry, protective, and concerned. She was upset that the kids had been mistreated and felt she had to intervene on their behalf. At the same time, she felt hopeless because her husband's drug use was getting worse and she didn't know what to do.

Ann wondered if she was going crazy. She knew it was normal and even appropriate to be upset about seeing her husband in a stupor on the couch, but she was puzzled by her feelings of severe depression.

Ann Remembers Her Childhood

Ann decided to seek out a counselor to help her deal with her depression. In the course of counseling, her counselor could see that Ann needed to get in touch with her child within to understand her feelings and heal the present problems. The counselor explained to Ann that her husband's worsening chemical dependency was activating some unresolved childhood issues. Her current situation was triggering feelings she had been trying to forget and hide.

Together, they used the early memory process to learn more about Ann's child within. Ann wrote down a memory of something that happened when she was 9: One day when she came home from school, the house was dark and quiet. Ann felt a strange sense of foreboding. Sometimes the house was filled with fun, laughter, and good feelings, but often it was like today: lonely, quiet, and empty. Ann remembered that she wanted to tell her mother about her exciting day at school and the fun she had at recess with her new best friend. Ann called out, but no one answered. She walked slowly into the living room and saw her father bending over her mother's slumped body.

"Daddy, Daddy," she cried out. "What's wrong? Is something wrong with Mommy?"

Ann's father looked up in great distress. "Honey, it's going to be OK," he said. "The ambulance is on the way and Mother is going to be OK. Help me get her up off the couch so we can carry her out to meet the ambulance."

Ann remembered that she felt both frightened and concerned. The vivid part of the memory was seeing her mother's slumped body. She decided that she might lose someone she really loved. Her fear eventually proved correct: Ann's mother attempted suicide many times. When Ann was 10, her mother finally succeeded in ending her life.

Ann's Parenting Was Affected by Unresolved Childhood Issues

Ann never realized that she had stored decisions and feelings from her early childhood and that these unconscious decisions were affecting her life. When Ann had children, she felt very protective of them. She didn't want to lose them, nor did she want them to experience the emotional pain that she felt as a child. Her mother had been available sometimes but emotionally unavailable at other times. Sometimes she'd be fun and happy, other times sharp-tongued and melancholy. Ann's father tried to make up for the loss, but the pain and anger of living with an "absent other" (a person who is there in body, but not in spirit) was too much for him.

When Ann's husband started behaving like her mother had, Ann was familiar with the pattern. Ann was used to others having mood shifts, though it scared her and increased her loneliness. Her husband's behavior activated her early belief that she might lose someone she loved.

David was a polydrug abuser, and his mood shifted depending on what he had taken. When he drank, he got really mellow and friendly and would be Mr. Nice Guy. Marijuana had the same effect on him. When he used cocaine, however, he'd get intense and out of touch with reality. He would spend time cleaning his desk and doing other things to escape from the family.

Ann alternated between overconcern for her children and overinvolvement with her husband's drug behavior. Sometimes she'd be so focused on David's behavior that she would completely ignore her kids. Other times she'd be more like her father and jump in and try to fix everything for the kids. Her meddling angered David, who said that he never got to work things through with the kids and that he could if she would just stay out of it.

Ann didn't feel good about what was going on or about herself. She was ashamed about her parenting, but felt addicted to nagging, meddling, and rescuing so her kids wouldn't have to suffer. It was obvious this wasn't working. However, like any other addictive person, Ann did more of what didn't work, hoping that eventually it would work.

Ann was repeating patterns from her childhood. Her father overprotected and rescued her when she was a child. She never learned to depend on herself or trust her judgment. When she had her family, she looked to her husband for leadership, but he was a drug abuser and had little leadership to offer. Ann's rage increased as her husband became more distant from the family.

Ann's anger turned to vengefulness as she tried to keep David away from the kids "to protect them." She continually put down his parenting methods in front of them. The children suffered from the dysfunction in the home. The children's teachers became concerned, noticing that the older girls were withdrawn and unhappy.

Ann Uses a "Magic Wand" to Heal Her Child Within

After her counselor helped her look back into her childhood, Ann realized that she had never worked through the pain and anger at her mother for abandoning her through suicide. She knew she was taking out her pain on the whole family.

Ann's counselor helped her continue the healing process. She suggested Ann go back to her childhood and pretend she had a magic wand powerful enough to change anything Ann wanted to in her early memory. Ann went back to the memory of her unconscious mother. She changed the memory so her mother would not be unconscious. Instead, her mother told Ann how she was feeling and what she was unhappy about. Her mother said she was going to get help with her problems so she could be there for Ann to help her grow up.

Ann began to cry just thinking about this wish. When she stopped crying, she said, "I know that my mother was unhappy for years before she committed suicide and that taking her life didn't mean she didn't love me. My mom was depressed for so long that she probably couldn't stand the pain anymore. There was nothing I could do to cheer her up. No matter how good I was, I was not the person who could cure my mother."

Ann made the connection between her magic wand wish and her current situation. She realized her husband's problems were not her fault and that she couldn't cure him. She was clear that he was depressed and hiding his feelings with drugs. She let go of the belief that it was up to her to fix her husband; instead, she focused on what she could do for herself.

In discovering her damaged "child within," Ann realized that the "little girl" inside thought her mother's depression was her fault. She tried to be very good so her mother would get better and she wouldn't be so lonely. Ann realized she was doing the same with her husband and it wouldn't work any better with him than with her mother.

Ann changed her thinking, feeling, and acting. She told herself it was up to her husband to seek help for his depression. Then she told him. She made the suggestion without nagging or expecting results. She was surprised at the powerful relief she felt by changing this one decision. She used her newfound energy to care for herself instead of caring for him.

The process of discovery can help change current behaviors as well as healing the pain from the past. Ann was able to heal the wounds experienced by her child within as well as to stop trying to run her husband's life. In our next story, we see how Bryce used discovery to change the way he parented his children.

Breaking the Cycle of Abusive Parenting Through Discovery

As a child, Bryce vowed he would never be the kind of parent his father was. Once he had children, he wanted to parent differently from the way his father had parented him, but he didn't know how.

Bryce was a polydrug abuser. His drug use was a way to disappear from the family and avoid his sense of failure. One day while Bryce was using drugs, he got into a physical fight with his 10-year-old son over the TV. Bryce decided he wouldn't let his son win this power struggle.

He sat on his son's head so he couldn't turn the TV back on.

In that moment, Bryce realized his patterns of dependence on drugs were keeping him parenting exactly the way his father had. He alternated between yelling and threatening the kids and then giving in by saying, "I don't care what you do, just get out of my sight!" He knew he needed help to learn how to parent and how to reparent himself. He wanted to stop laying all his old baggage on his kids. This realization gave Bryce the motivation to get help from NA, and to stop using drugs.

At an NA meeting, Bryce listened while others talked about physical abuses they suffered as kids. Bryce's father had been physically abusive with him. It was painful for Bryce to realize he was doing the same thing with his kids. He decided he would find a better way to deal with his anger than to use drugs, to leave the situation, or to abuse his son while under the influence.

When Bryce faced his failure as a parent, he realized that it wasn't enough just to stop using drugs to change his parenting style. Becoming a respectful parent would take time and skill building. With the help of his therapist, Bryce decided to do some discovery through early memory work, to learn more about his inner child.

Bryce remembered when he was 10 and his parents gave a party for their friends. They thought it would be cute to let Bryce be the bartender, dressed up in a little suit and tie. Bryce didn't know how to make drinks, so he was very generous with the alcohol proportions and several people got drunk.

Bryce thought he'd done a good job because he got so many compliments from the people at the party about his great drinks. He felt a sense of accomplishment and decided there was at least one thing he could do that was acceptable to his father—he could pour a drink.

Bryce remembered liking the sound of adult chit-chat and drunk people crowded around the bar. He enjoyed being busy taking care of their drink orders. When his dad said, "Pour 2 ounces," Bryce poured a little more. Bryce liked having a job and taking part. He felt he had belonging and significance in the drinking and partying lifestyle.

Understanding this early memory gave Bryce many insights about how his present behavior was related to his early decisions. He realized that the 10-year-old boy inside him still wanted to be invited to take part in things going on around him. He wanted to be complimented and recognized for his contribution.

He also realized that what had made him popular as a kid was not following directions. When he realized this, he decided to tell his wife about it. He also asked her if she would be more complimentary when he participated in the family. He suggested that it would be better if she were not to give him directions but instead to ask for help.

It helped Bryce understand his son better after he got in touch, in his early memory work, with how much he disliked being told what to do. Bryce realized that a lot of the confrontations he had with his son were because he was trying to control his son and order him around. Bryce decided to stop trying to control his son's behavior and concentrate on controlling his own behavior.

He thought back to the power struggle with his son over the TV and decided that in the future he would not try to work things out with his son in the heat of a battle. He could walk away and cool off instead of being physical with his son. When they had both calmed down, they could work together to find a solution that showed respect for both of them. This was the beginning of his efforts to learn behaviors that would be respectful to himself and his son.

Bryce wanted to take part as a contributing member of his family. When he was using, he didn't give himself that chance. He had alienated them with his abusive behavior. They were used to him being a bully or a wimp. It would take time before they trusted him to follow through with dignity and respect.

At the suggestion of his therapist, Bryce decided to attend some parenting classes. He was eager to learn new skills so he could stop dealing with his anger by exploding and creating scenes as his father had done.

Bryce was amazed at the positive results the family experienced from family meetings. The family meeting time became a time when the whole family could help work things out together. They could talk openly about their problems and their feelings. Bryce learned to list things that bothered him on the family meeting agenda, instead of trying to solve them by himself in the moment of struggle. He learned to tell his kids when he felt angry and to ask for their help to work out solutions they all could live with. Everyone else did the same. He could feel trust building in the family.

The process of discovery and early memory work was instrumental in helping both Bryce and Ann change their dysfunctional patterns of behavior and heal their hurt feelings. In the next situation, we see how Lisa used the early memory process to work on her trust issues.

The Process of Discovery Uncovers the Origins of Trust Issues

Lisa and Steve met in recovery and decided to live together. Lisa couldn't understand why she was so cold to Steve's

4-year-old daughter or why she didn't trust her even though Jenna was so adorable. Through the discovery process and early memory work, Lisa was able to recognize the game she was playing with her stepdaughter and to stop it.

Lisa thought of an early memory when she was 11. She said, "My stepfather had to travel a lot and was out of town. When he'd go out of town, my mother and I got along better. It was summer, and my stepsister was there. Mom had a friend come stay with us because she hated staying alone. They got drunk. My sister and I snuck some wine and started drinking.

"We were sitting in the living room quietly listening to them talk. Mom wasn't being obnoxious, like she normally was when she was drunk. Then we heard Mom and her friend crawling up the stairs because they couldn't walk. We were laughing at them. My mother stuck her head through the bars of the banister, and my stepsister laughed, but I had this sick, repulsed feeling in my stomach. I thought Mom was the most disgusting person alive."

The vivid part of Lisa's memory was seeing her mother's head sticking through the bars on the stairs. The unconscious decision she made at that time was, "No matter if we were getting along or not, I could never fully trust her. I could never know when she would do something disgusting."

Lisa didn't realize she was deciding she couldn't trust people who appeared to be nice. Unconsciously she decided that underneath the "nice" lurks a mean and obnoxious person. When Lisa met Steve's "nice" 4-year-old daughter, she had no idea that she was applying the decision she made about her mother to the child.

It took Lisa about six months to establish a trusting relationship with Jenna after discovering her hidden beliefs, but she felt highly motivated to improve their relationship. Steve's coaxing and pressuring didn't help get his daughter and Lisa together. It did help when Lisa used information from her past to discover her own distrustful little girl within. She could then make new decisions more appropriate for the present.

Lisa still has trust issues, but she realizes her lack of trust is a statement about her and not necessarily about the "nice" people she can't trust. She has more work to do in this area, but she feels good about the steps she has taken with Jenna.

Healing the Child Within

Another way to heal the inner child involves role-playing an early childhood memory and then replaying the memory the way we would like it to be. Through this process, we can come experientially to different conclusions about ourselves.

Nancy was an adult child of an alcoholic. She was afraid of having an outburst that would harm her relationships. Nancy had been blaming her "3-year-old" inner child for all the problems that happened in her family of origin. After her therapist pointed out how cruel she was being to her child within, Nancy decided to try a role-play in one of her therapy sessions.

When Nancy was growing up, the family atmosphere was like a war zone. Nancy's father, John, was aggressive, vindictive, abusive, and tyrannical. She spent all her time in her room because she was either hiding or sent there. Nancy's mother Pat would be "helpful." She'd clean up John's vomit and the ashes in the fireplace after he urinated on them, and she'd make sure John had clean clothes for work.

With sarcasm and anger in her voice, Nancy remarked, "We never had 'a problem.' Nobody talked about my father's alcoholism. All Mother ever did was make excuses for my father's behavior. Everything was focused on that."

Nancy needed encouragement before she agreed to think of a childhood memory to replay. Thinking about her childhood was so painful that Nancy preferred to avoid it. She overcame her resistance because she wanted to get better and believed early memory work would help.

Nancy shared the following early memory: "My mom and I are coming down the street. We want to go in the front door of the house and it's locked. We know my dad's in there, so we go around to the back. The back door is open, but he gets there first and doesn't want us to come in. He's pushing the door shut. My mom pushes the door open, and we go in. He starts throwing pots and pans at her, and it becomes loud and confusing. I don't remember anymore. I probably split. I was 3 or 4. The vivid part of the memory is a pan going across the room and hitting Mom's leg."

When asked what decision she made at the time, Nancy said, "I decided I was pretty helpless and there was nothing I could do to help. Now, when I feel helpless, I decide I can wait indefinitely and can get away with not dealing with something. My hope is that everything will be OK if I just avoid it. It's only when it starts nagging at me or I think about it all day that I have to think about dealing with it."

Nancy could see how her childhood affected her parenting. She shared an incident where her 15-year-old son was using the remote control to change channels while she was watching TV. She got out of the chair and went to grab the remote, forgetting how big her son was. As she rushed at him, he pushed her shoulder and she went sprawling across the room. She screamed and then watched as her son went into his room and took the remote with him. She went into her avoidance mode and waited till the remote was returned. It took a day.

Nancy said, "I'm so scared of being belligerent like my dad that I hold things in and avoid dealing with them until they really get bad."

Nancy Acts Out Her Childhood Memory

Nancy decided to role-play herself. Her therapist pretended to be her belligerent father throwing the pan. In the middle of the role-play, Nancy broke down in tears. She had been holding so much pain inside, and the crying was a huge release. After the tears, Nancy got in touch with how much anger she feels toward her dad after all these years. When she had the opportunity to replay the memory the way she wished it had been, she used her "magic wand" to go back and let her father know how angry and hurt she felt.

Nancy's rage came out with shouts and physical violence (against a pillow that represented her dad). The release of these feelings left Nancy feeling lighter than she had in years and less afraid of having an outburst in real life. The role-playing opened the door for Nancy to continue in her healing and growing.

Nancy Learns to Speak Gently to Her Child Within

Nancy's therapist asked her if she could think of any children she knew who were 3 or 4 years old, the age she had been when the violent episode occurred. Nancy immediately thought of one of her favorite nieces. The therapist asked Nancy what she would do if that child experienced a scene like Nancy had described. Nancy was quick to say she'd pick the little girl up, hold her, comfort her, and tell her that she was going to be OK and that it wasn't her fault. It had never occurred to Nancy that the little girl inside her also needed the same kind of acceptance and love. The therapist asked Nancy to imagine putting the little girl within on her lap and giving her the love she needed. When Nancy did this, she felt much love for her little girl within. This image has persisted and has often helped Nancy when she felt discouraged.

When she is having a problem, Nancy uses the discovery technique to think of an early childhood memory, to see if she can figure out how old her "inner child" might be in those moments. Then she thinks about what would most encourage such a child, and the healing begins.

Encouraging and Healing Yourself

Healing your child within is a powerful way to encourage yourself. If you would like to try healing your child within through early memory work, try the following activity:

1. When you feel discouraged, think of an early memory. When you have the memory clearly in your mind, ask yourself what you are feeling and what decision you are making in that memory. Make sure you include your age in the memory, to help you know how old your "inner child" is with whom you are dealing.

2. Think of the situation that is making you feel discouraged now. What are your feelings and decisions? Are they similar to the feelings and decisions in your early memory?

3. Pretend you have a magic wand and can change your early memory any way you want. What changes would you make? What would you do differently, or what would others do differently to make things turn out better?

4. If you changed your early memory by doing something different, try doing the same thing to change your present situation. If you changed your early memory by having someone else do something different, think about how you might encourage someone else to make those same changes. You might be surprised how effective it is to simply tell someone what you want. However, you can't change another person if he or she doesn't want to change. If you can't get what you want from someone else, use your imagination to give it to yourself.

Discovery through early memory work can be powerful in helping us learn about the unconscious decisions that motivate our feelings and behavior. Healing takes place when we use this process to encourage ourselves, and to discover new decisions and new behaviors that are respectful to ourselves and others.

Chapter

12

Encourage Yourself and Others

Addicts will lie, cheat, and steal to protect their using. They make promises they never keep, yet co-dependent members of the family keep hoping "this time" it will be different. If someone in your family is abusing chemicals, you may feel you are living in a nightmare.

There are many discouraging patterns and behaviors that are part of chemically dependent relationships. You may share the discouragement of many co-dependents who *hope* that things will improve, but who never *take action* to make changes. The behaviors of the addict and the co-dependent feed on each other, and the nightmare gets worse. It may seem overwhelming and impossible to change.

Encouragement—the process of building courage—can help you break abusive cycles for yourself and others. This does not mean you can use encouragement to change another person. You can use encouragement to change yourself or to provide an environment where others may be inspired to examine their behavior because they know they will not be judged. Examination can lead to awareness, and awareness can lead to change. Examination, awareness, and change are unlikely to occur in an environment where people do not feel encouraged.

When people feel encouraged, they can handle any situation with dignity and respect for themselves and others. The key to dignity and respect is honoring what you think, what you feel, and what you want without expecting anyone else to think the same, feel the same, or give you what you want. Before you can honor what you think, feel, and want, you have to know what you think, feel, and want. It is not likely that you will know what you think, feel, and want unless your thoughts, feelings, and wants are treated with dignity and respect.

Learning to act with dignity and respect takes practice. It doesn't happen overnight, but people get good at whatever they practice. You can continue practicing old behaviors of co-dependency and discouragement, or you can learn and practice new behaviors that stop the discouragement cycle. Practicing dignity and respect creates a cycle of encouragement instead of discouragement.

Eleven Skills for Encouraging Yourself and Others with Dignity and Respect

1. *Accept the reality of what is* instead of living in denial by acting as though people and situations will fulfill your dreams.

2. *Trust people to be who they are* instead of who you want them to be.

3. *Pay attention to what people do* instead of to what they say they will do.

4. *Understand feelings, accept feelings, and practice emotional honesty* instead of avoiding or discounting feelings.

5. *Decide what you will do* instead of trying to get others to do what you want them to do.

6. *Learn skills to improve co-parenting* even when separated or divorced.

7. *Take the initiative to create what you want with dignity and respect for yourself and others* instead of feeling like a victim because others don't give you what you want.

8. *Validate yourself* when you don't get validation from others.

9. *Create successes by using encouragement* instead of praise.

10. *Take time to practice new skills of encouragement* instead of expecting perfection immediately.

11. *Fill your own cup* instead of seeking fulfillment from outside yourself.

Encouraging Yourself and Others with Dignity and Respect

Mandy and Mack were in a lying-hoping, emotionally abusive relationship that flourished through his addiction and her co-dependency. Mack was a closet drinker. Although there was tension and a lack of communication in Mandy's home, she didn't realize her husband was an alcoholic. She was sure the kids didn't pick up on what was going on, either. According to Mandy, her husband Mack didn't show any outward signs of alcohol abuse. They never fought. There was just a lot of silence.

As their relationship deteriorated, Mack became more abusive with the kids. One day he showed up at a neighborhood party drunk. His kids were antsy and acting up, so Mack slapped one of the kids across the head and said, "Knock it off!" Everyone at the party turned around and looked. Mandy felt shocked and embarrassed. She didn't know what to do.

Mack took off in the pouring rain by himself. In typical co-dependent style, Mandy borrowed a car, threw the kids in, and drove around looking for him. When she couldn't find him, she went home. Later he came home and said he was sorry. Mandy hoped everything would be better and believed Mack's promise when he said he wouldn't let his drinking get out of hand again.

Patterns from the Past

The patterns of hope and denial Mandy had learned from her childhood home were being repeated in her marriage. When she grew up, her father was an alcoholic, but Mandy had never heard that word used to describe what was happening in her family. Her father was quiet and withdrawn except when drunk. Then he'd become verbally abusive. Mandy's mother would make snide remarks behind his back but never addressed anything directly to him. No one admitted that he was an alcoholic.

Mandy thought her mother was mean for picking on her father. Mandy excused his drinking because he spoiled her and favored her, and she pretended it wasn't really such a big problem. She thought this was how everyone lived.

It was easy for Mandy to pretend her father didn't drink because he never drank in front of anyone. Yet she admitted she had always known that he drank in secret. He kept bottles hidden in the garage and under the front seat of the car.

When Mandy was about 9, she got mad at her father one day because he broke a promise and disappointed her. Because she was angry at her father, Mandy cleaned out the garage and went through the cupboards. She found more than thirty empty bottles of vodka, which she lined up on the dining room table. When her father woke up, she confronted him. He hung his head and left the room while Mandy was still yelling and screaming that alcohol was more important to him than she was. When he left, she felt helpless.

From this experience, Mandy concluded she was helpless against alcoholism. She also decided people she loved would leave her, as her father had, if she created a confrontation. It was less painful for Mandy to pretend her father wasn't an alcoholic than to face life without him.

In her marriage to Mack, that pattern repeated itself. Mandy and Mack found an ill-informed marriage counselor who reinforced their beliefs by saying Mack really didn't have an alcohol problem because he had never been picked up for drunk driving. Mandy was able to find many people who helped her maintain her denial and run her relationship on wishful thinking.

Mack cooperated in the deception by pretending everything was OK, drinking in secret, and hiding from Mandy his true feelings about the relationship. He avoided his kids and spent hours sitting silently in a chair staring at the wall. When things got out of hand, he'd promise not to let it happen again.

The whole family was extremely discouraged.

Encouragement Skill No. 1: Accept the Reality of What Is

One day in the therapist's office Mack announced that he was leaving Mandy. Her reaction was complete fear and panic. She yelled, "If you think you're going to stick me with the kids, you're out of your mind!"

Once she recovered from the shock, the crisis motivated Mandy to get into recovery and deal with her denial and co-dependency. It wasn't an easy process for Mandy to admit that her husband was an alcoholic and that alcohol had been ruining their lives. Her Al-Anon group helped her face her most immediate problem—single parenting.

Mandy thought single parenting would be overwhelming and that she couldn't handle it. Her fears were not justified. She was surprised to find that life got easier for her when she gave up denial and faced reality. She stopped hoping someone else would change and started looking at what she could do to improve her life. Her worst fear, that someone would leave her, had already occurred. She found that being alone was better than feeling alone and living in fear and denial. Because of her fear of being left, she had settled for a life with an "absent other," a mate who brings his body to the relationship, but not himself. Mack was either under the influence or focusing on his drug to the exclusion of everyone else in his life. No wonder Mandy felt so alone while in a "relationship."

After the separation, Mandy found a different therapist and joined a parenting class with some members of her Al-Anon group. Her first step in breaking the cycle of living on lies and passive hope was to be more honest with her kids. She let the secret out about Mack: she discussed the fact that their father was an alcoholic. Even as she told the kids, she heard the old voices in her head saying, "This isn't true, and it's not that bad." It was hard for her to give up her pattern of believing Mack's promises to control his drinking.

Encouragement Skill No. 2:
Trust People to Be Who They Are

"But I trusted you!" is a common declaration we hear from people who feel their trust has been betrayed.

Usually, these people have a mistaken understanding of the meaning of trust.

When we say we trust others, does that mean we trust them to be who they are, or does it mean we trust them to be who we want them to be? To trust another person to be who we want them to be is a setup for disappointment and discouragement.

In her heart, Mandy was relieved that Mack's alcoholism was finally out of the closet. Understanding the truth helped her and the kids trust Mack to be who he was instead of who they wanted him to be. It also helped Mandy break the cycle of denial that started in her family of origin.

When Mandy trusted Mack to be who he was, she stopped criticizing him and trying to change his parenting style. This created an unexpected benefit for Mandy after the divorce. Mack became much more involved with the kids when he felt encouraged instead of discouraged by all the criticism, and Mandy didn't have to be so alone as a parent.

When the kids learned to trust their dad to be who he was, they started sticking up for themselves. When Mack made promises, they said, "Don't make promises unless you intend to keep them." Mack continued to break promises, but the kids decided they wanted to spend some time with him anyway. When they complained about his broken promises, Mandy reminded them, "That is part of what your dad does. How do you want to handle it?" She helped them work out a plan to handle their disappointment. They decided to make alternate plans and told their dad they would wait fifteen minutes for him to show up. If he was fifteen minutes late, they would follow their alternate plan.

As frightening and painful as it is to face reality, it is less painful than living with lies and passive hope.

An important step leading out of denial is to trust people to be who they are instead of who you want them to be, and to make plans for what *you* will do instead of what you will try making *them* do. This eliminates the disappointment and despair perpetuated in the cycle of lies, broken promises, and passive hope for change. Trusting people to be who they are is an important step in the encouragement process. Another step is to "listen" to behavior instead of words.

Encouragement Skill No. 3:
Pay Attention to What People Do

If you want to understand people, pay more attention to what they do than to what they say. Watch their tongues. The tongues in their mouths (words) may say one thing while the tongues in their shoes (actions) give a different message. People may convey good intentions with their words, but their actions tell us the truth about what they are doing.

Alfred Adler said repeatedly, "Watch the movement, not the words." People often say one thing and then do something else. The proof of the pudding is in the behavior. Actions do speak louder than words.

People move toward healthy communication when words and actions are congruent. When the tongues in their mouths and their shoes match, people are being respectful and encouraging to themselves and others. When their messages go in different directions, our communication becomes filled with double messages.

Listening to the difference between words and behavior is another key for getting out of the cycle of lies, denial, and passive hope. Learning the skill of trusting behavior instead of words helped Mandy strengthen her way out of denial and started a spiral of en*courage*ment.

The Encouragement of Trusting Behavior

Mandy wanted the boys to have time with their father, and she wanted help with the kids. While in denial, she had lived in a constant state of frustration and disappointment because Mack didn't live up to any of her hopes and dreams. Mandy felt like she was parenting everybody: her three young boys *and* her husband.

When Mandy finally paid more attention to Mack's behavior than to his words or her expectations, she was able to stop denying that he was dependent on chemicals. After their divorce, Mack did not spend any time with the kids for over a year.

When Mack finally took an interest in spending time with his kids, it took a while for Mandy to practice the advice of her counselor about giving more credibility to what Mack did than to what he said. She made many mistakes while learning. In the beginning, she would ask Mack if he had quit drinking, and he would say yes he had. Mandy's feelings told her to be careful, but she didn't listen to her feelings. Instead, she listened to Mack's words.

Encouragement Skill No. 4:
Understand Feelings, Accept Feelings, and Practice Emotional Honesty

Later the kids would come home with stories about their father's drinking, drunk driving, and verbal abuse. Mandy knew she should trust her feelings about the building evidence of his alcohol abuse. She was especially concerned that the children might not be safe with him. Even so, it was difficult for her to tell the kids they couldn't see their father. It was easier for her to believe Mack's words than to take a stand and let him know that he couldn't spend time alone with the boys when he was drinking.

213

One afternoon, one of the boys needed a ride home from the library. He couldn't reach his mom, so he called his dad and asked for a ride. When his father started talking, the 10-year-old knew his dad was drunk. He felt scared and said, "Don't come, Dad. I see Mom's car outside the door." Then he slammed down the phone.

When her son finally reached Mandy on the phone, he told her how scared and uncomfortable he was. Mandy said, "Your father is an alcoholic, and you did the right thing. You do not have to get in a car with him when he is drunk. I'm sorry it was so frightening for you, but I'm glad that you called me." Mandy felt relieved because they were treating Mack's drinking as a reality and the kids were learning skills to take care of themselves.

Honesty is a key component of encouragement. It was an important step for Mandy to trust her feelings and make it clear to her son that he could trust his feelings. This encouraged her son to know that he used his judgment and power constructively when he followed his feelings and said no to his dad.

Mandy had many oportunities to practice listening to Mack's behavior instead of his words. She became more aware that he often did not "walk his talk," and that the tongue in his shoe often went in a different direction from the tongue in his mouth. Mandy knew she couldn't make Mack stop drinking, and she couldn't make him tell the truth. However, she *could* admit reality to herself and to the kids.

Shortly after Mack's alcoholism was discussed openly, he began to attend AA meetings and started his recovery process. Mandy's move out of denial began the process that led him to that decision. Ironically Mack chose for himself what he had resisted as long as he felt pushed by Mandy.

Recovery Is Not the End of the Rainbow

Mandy was surprised at how discouraged she felt when Mack went into recovery. She felt overburdened and angry about being the only parent while Mack was drinking, and she believed recovery would be the solution to all her problems. She thought Mack would now share equal responsibility with the kids. Instead, he was too involved in his recovery program to spend time with them. He spent all his free time at AA meetings. She saw Mack getting all kinds of praise and encouragement for his involvement in AA. It seemed to her that he had free rein to be selfish, while she still had full responsibility for the kids. Mandy was also angry and resentful because Mack waited until he left to get his life together.

Mandy isn't the only recovering parent who has these feelings. Many recovering people wait patiently for their spouses to stop using or drinking. They believe that the minute their spouses go into recovery things will be magically changed. They expect them to become fully involved in co-parenting. Instead they spend five nights a week at AA meetings and other activities not related to alcohol.

Mandy could have spent the rest of her life feeling frustrated and bitter because her expectations did not come true. Instead, she learned the value of acting instead of reacting. She learned to decide what she would do.

Encouragement Skill No. 5: Decide What You Will Do

Mandy had practiced using her encouragement skills enough to catch herself falling into old patterns of wanting things to be different but thinking that she had no power to make them change. She could see she needed more practice at accepting the reality of what is. She decided to practice the skill of acting instead of reacting. She focused on what she could do instead of focusing on her disappointment that Mack wasn't living up to her expectations. Her parenting class helped her learn more skills that focused on what she could do.

When one of the boys came home with a note from the teacher saying he had been fighting at school, Mandy decided what she would do. In the past, she would have called Mack and insisted he do something about his son's behavior and that it was his fault their son was getting in trouble. This time she sat down with her son, asked him to tell her about what happened, and asked if he needed help working this out with his teacher. She felt satisfied when he said that he thought he could handle it himself. Whenever she was unsure if she had done enough, Mandy went to her parenting class and used the group to get a reality check. She gave up counting on her ex-husband to make things right.

While they were both in recovery, Mandy from co-dependency and Mack from alcohol abuse, they faced another problem. Mandy and Mack did not have effective co-parenting skills while they were married. Now they wanted to be co-parents while divorced and in recovery. They were like many other people in recovery who have limited skills to work effectively with a spouse, ex-spouse, or a blended family.

Encouragement Skill No. 6: Learn Skills to Improve Co-Parenting

Although there are difficulties for children of divorce, Mandy learned many possibilities for working through her co-parenting problems in an encouraging and respectful way with her ex-spouse. She could see the positive aspects for divorced parents. Her kids had two extended families who cared about them. They had the opportunity to deal with two different parenting styles. She had free time and independence when the kids were with their dad. An added benefit was the opportunity for the kids to observe their parents heal from circumstances that can break a family. They learned it is possible to grow stronger from tough times.

In her parenting education class, Mandy learned to treat her kids honestly, divide responsibilities, and have them participate through family meetings. She was delighted to discover that the skills she learned in her parenting class also helped her improve her relationship with Mack and their co-parenting skills. She gained more practice in dealing with Mack honestly. She invited him to participate in some family meetings to discuss problems of mutual concern, and she spoke honestly with Mack about dividing responsibilities with the kids.

Although they are still divorced, Mandy says her relationship with Mack is wonderful now. He spends time with the kids regularly until he starts feeling guilty about the damage he thinks he did to his children. He then avoids contact with them instead of facing his guilt and letting go of the past.

Mandy feels frustrated when he goes into his avoidance routine, but doesn't waste much time feeling helpless. She uses her new skills to create what she wants with respect.

Encouragement Skill No. 7:
Take the Initiative to Create What
You Want with Dignity and Respect
for Yourself and Others

Mandy has learned that the recovering spouse needs encouragement to keep trying. Instead of scolding or lecturing when Mack backs out of the picture, Mandy understands and acts appropriately. She calls Mack and offers several suggestions for ways he could spend time with the kids. He seems relieved and chooses several of her suggestions. When Mandy trusts Mack to be who he is, she initiates contact between him and the kids because she knows he does not think ahead.

Mandy still worries about her ability to earn money as a single parent. Sometimes she finds herself resenting that she didn't have the family of her dreams. When she hears that inner voice, she remembers that wishing for things caused much pain and that facing reality has enhanced her life. She then decides to act with dignity and respect to change what she can change instead of acting like a victim.

Encouragement Skill No. 8: Validate Yourself

One of the most healing things that happened for Mandy was when Mack asked her to go to AA one night when he spoke. When he said, "I destroyed my family and my relationship, and I hurt my kids," she cried. She felt validated for all she had done and could appreciate Mack's courage in involving her at that meeting.

Some of us may never experience that kind of validation from someone else. Ideally, it is best if the person who has wronged or misunderstood us is the person who lets us know they understand and affirm us now. Sometimes that can't happen because the person has died or is still using. Other times there is so much pain and past resentment that the parties involved aren't ready to help each other heal hurt feelings. They are not far enough into their recovery to make amends. Sometimes people simply don't have the awareness and skills to make up for their mistakes. In those cases, people need to seek the validation from friends, counselors, other family members, or at twelve-step meetings.

In counseling, we role-play with clients, pretending to be the absent other and telling clients what they need to hear. At other times, we invite clients to talk to an empty chair and ask for affirmation. Then we have the clients switch to sit in the empty chair and say what they wish they could hear from someone else. Sometimes it's enough for them to acknowledge that they wish the perpetrator of hurt could say he or she is sorry and show understanding.

In a recent session, a client was wishing her ex-husband could say, "I don't know how or why you hung in there with me when I was blowing all the family's money. I bet that was really upsetting and scary for you. You must have pulled rabbits out of hats to keep the family in food and shelter while I was busy with my addictive behavior. Thank you."

This client knows she is not likely to hear these words from her ex-husband, but decided she deserves to hear them and asked her therapist to say them to her.

Validation can come from within or from friendly sources when we understand that the person we want validation from isn't capable. The important thing is that we deserve validation, not mistreatment.

The first eight skills for encouragement show many ways to use honesty instead of denial, to respect yourself and others, and to act instead of react. The last four skills for encouragement show you how to build for the future through encouragement with children and how to practice and learn from mistakes. Many specific skills promote healing and growth through the art of encouragement with children. The bonus you get when you use encouragement with children is that it helps you learn to encourage yourself.

Encouragement Skill No. 9:
Create Successes by Using Encouragement

Recovery is enhanced when people learn the difference between praise and encouragement. Praise teaches children to depend on the external judgments of others, instead of trusting their internal wisdom and self-evaluation. A steady diet of praise inspires children to believe, "I'm OK only if others say I'm OK." It also teaches them to avoid mistakes instead of to learn from their mistakes.

The chart on page 221 shows more about the differences between praise and encouragement.

It's easy to encourage someone who is doing what you think is good for them. But what can you say to the kid who is misbehaving and not feeling good about him- or herself? For example, when Timmy brings home A's and B's on his report card, it's easy to say, "You're doing so well. You must feel very good about that." But what happens when Timmy brings home D's and F's? He still needs his parents' feedback. An encouraging parent might say, "Timmy, I'm concerned about these grades. Can you tell me more about how this happened and how you feel about it?"

Encouraging parents practice mutual respect without judgment. They respect themselves enough to share their thoughts and feelings, but don't assume, without asking, what kids are thinking and feeling.

In the chemically dependent family, the focus is on covering up feelings and not paying attention to internal messages. When you encourage instead of praise your kids, you are teaching them to listen to their thoughts and feelings.

In Kitty's family, learning the difference between praise and encouragement was useful to encourage their oldest daughter, who had taken on the role of family hero. While

Differences Between Praise and Encouragement

	Praise	Encouragement
Webster's Dictionary Definition	1. To express a favorable *judgment* of 2. To glorify, especially by attribution of *perfection*	1. To inspire with courage 2. To spur on: *stimulate*
Recognizes	Only complete, perfect product	Effort and improvement
Attitude	Patronizing, manipulative	Respectful, appreciative
"I" Message	Judgmental: "I like the way you are sitting."	Self-disclosing: "I appreciate your cooperation."
Used Most Often with	Children: "You're such a good little girl"	Adults: "Thanks for helping."
Examples	"I'm proud of you for getting an A in math." (robs person of ownership of own achievement)	"That A reflects your hard work." (recognizes ownership and responsibility for achievement)
Invites	People to change for others	People to change for themselves
Locus of Control	External: "What do you think?"	Internal: "What do I think?"
Teaches	What to think	How to think
Goal	Conformity: "You did it right."	Understanding: "What do you think, feel, learn?"
Effect on Self-Esteem	Feel worthwhile only when others approve	Feel worthwhile without others' approval
Long-Range Effect	Dependence on others	Self-confidence; self-reliance

Source: Revised from a chart by Bonnie G. Smith and Judy Dixon.

Kitty's husband was in early recovery, Kitty joined a parenting class and decided that she would work on statements of encouragement instead of praise. When her daughter came to her and asked, "Aren't you proud of me?" Kitty would ask, "How do you feel?" or say, "Seems like you're really proud of yourself. What you think and feel is important to me."

Kitty's daughter was motivated by the need to please others instead of herself. Kitty said, "I want her to take care of herself and to know herself. Learning about the difference between praise and encouragement has given me a tool where I can help accomplish that."

Many people are skilled at praise and criticism, but have not had much practice with encouragement. You may find it helpful to practice using encouraging statements similar to those in the following examples:[1]

- *Express gratitude:* "Thank you. I appreciate what you did."
- *Focus on skills:* "Now you can play pretty music for all of us."
- *Use empathy:* "I'll bet that was fun."
- *Let them know the impact of their behavior:* "When you water the plants, I have more time to play with you."
- *Stress uniqueness:* "We sure see things differently, don't we?"
- *Acknowledge effort:* "I can see much work went into this."
- *Label the act:* "We're having an argument."
- *Practice acceptance:* "You hate it when we argue, and you wish we would stop."

---

[1]A summary of information from a workshop with John Taylor, author of *Person to Person* (Saratoga, CA: R & E Publishers, 1984) and *Helping Your Hyperactive Child* (Rocklin, CA: Prima, 1990).

Encouragement Skill No. 10: Take Time to Practice New Skills of Encouragement

Rudolph Dreikurs said, "Children need encouragement like a plant needs water." Encouragement is a process of showing the kind love that conveys to children that they are good enough the way they are. It teaches children that what they do is separate from who they are. Encouragement lets children know they are valued for their uniqueness without judgment. Through encouragement, parents teach children that mistakes are simply opportunities to learn and grow instead of something of which to be ashamed. Children who feel encouraged have self-love and feel a sense of belonging and uniqueness.

A primary facet of love and encouragement is mutual respect. Mutual respect means loving and respecting yourself, and loving and respecting your kids. It is almost impossible to learn courage and self-love in an environment that lacks mutual respect. In our zeal to mold our children "for their own good," we often forget to be respectful.

Adults are disrespectful and discouraging to children in many ways, without realizing it. Any form of punishment or permissiveness is disrespectful and discouraging to children. Parents are disrespectful when they don't take time to *get into the child's world* to understand differences and appreciate uniqueness. Yet even though adults are often disrespectful to children, they insist that children show respect to adults. Does this make sense?

An important part of respect and encouragement is honoring people's right to control their own behavior. Will people ever learn that the only behavior they can control is their own? Adults may be able to make children *act* respectful, but they can't make kids *feel* respectful. The best way to encourage them to *feel* respectful is for adults to control their own behavior and model respect for themselves and for others.

People are not born with the ability to be encouraging. It is a skill that takes practice. Sometimes it helps to set up a special time each day to practice the art of encouragement. The following activity helps parents succeed in practicing mutual respect through encouragement. We suggest you pick a time to do this activity once a week or once a day, to increase your skills.

"Just for Today" Activity This activity helps keep expectations realistic. Say to yourself, *"Just for today I will be gentle with myself in my new way of life. I will celebrate successes and learn from mistakes."* One way to celebrate success and learn from mistakes is to take time to go over the following possibilities. You may want to complete the sentences in your mind, or take time to complete the sentences in a journal.

- *One problem I had with parenting today was*
- *One successful parenting experience I had today was*
- *I did or did not take time to listen in the following ways*
- *I was or was not kind when I set limits because*
- *I was or was not consistent in the following ways*
- *I was or was not encouraging in the following ways*
- *I did or did not show respect for myself by*
- *I did or did not show respect for my family members by*
- *Here is an example of what happened when I did or did not share my feelings*
- *I withdrew from conflict in the following situation*
- *I took time for fun*
- *Just for today I learned*

Remember the wisdom of the following phrases: One day at a time. Keep it simple. Easy does it. Have the courage to be imperfect. Recovery is a process.

Encouragement Activity This activity for practicing encouragement helps parents focus on doing one thing at a time. Finish the following sentence: *I noticed my child was discouraged when*

And choose one of the following items to finish this sentence: *One thing I will do to encourage him or her is*

1. *Say how I feel.*
2. *Ask how he or she feels.*
3. *Give a hug.*
4. *Smile.*
5. *Use an encouraging message.*
6. *Think of a time when I was a kid and felt discouraged. What would I have liked the adults to do? I'll do that for my child.*
7. *Be empathic while allowing my child to experience the consequences of his or her behavior without rescuing, scolding, or fixing.*
8. *Come from my heart and create my own methods of encouragement.*

Encouragement Skill No. 11: Fill Your Own Cup

It's hard to be an encouraging person if you're not taking care of yourself. Take time to list the things that fill your cup and then plan time to include these things in your life. Some ideas include taking a bath, going to a meeting, calling a friend, reading a book, sitting down and putting your feet up, listening to music, going out for an ice cream cone, getting a massage, or going for a long walk.

Many people get overloaded with the tasks of recovery. They forget to leave time for themselves or time for fun. Some don't know how to have fun without the aid of substances.

Is the texture of your day the way you want it? If not, it's up to you to decide what you will do to make it better. Waiting for someone else to make you happy is magical thinking.

It's OK to ask for help, but other people aren't mind readers. You need to be clear about the kind of help you want. The more specific you can be, the greater your chances of getting what you want. When you encourage yourself and fill your own cup, encouraging others will then follow through with ease.

Chapter

13

Face Your Fears, Share Your Shame, and Give Up Guilt

A major difference between parents in recovery and other parents is the recovering parents' feelings of guilt and shame. It is hard for former users to erase their memories of driving the kids to a ball game in a blackout, having the kids sit in the car for hours while they were in the bar, noticing the kids watching from the doorway while they were snorting cocaine, and forgetting to show up for their kids' birthday parties or showing up drunk. Many parents experience terrible guilt and shame for sexually and physically abusing their kids while under the influence. Some got in trouble with the law while they were using or had the police come to their door to arrest them for traffic violations, shoplifting, and other crimes while their kids watched from the sidelines.

Recovering parents may be racked with feelings of guilt and grief when they realize how much they focused on a drug or on a drug abuser instead of nurturing their children. The sense of loss can be overwhelming, and self-loathing is common.

There is no question that children of using parents have suffered immensely. That cannot be undone—but you can make changes in the present. Guilt and shame do not help children. What children want and need are parents who can show them how to recover from the past and live loving, responsible lives now. This requires effective parenting skills.

Good Intentions Are Not Enough

Although parents in recovery often have good intentions to make changes and have their family life be different, without new skills nothing they do seems good enough and the changes are elusive. At this point, feelings of failure are added to their guilt and shame. Nonproductive thoughts, feelings, and actions get in the way of effective parenting in the present. The challenge for parents in recovery is to break the cycle of fear, shame, and guilt by changing their thoughts, their feelings, or their actions.

Keys to Change

Actions are motivated by feelings. Feelings are created by thoughts. People's thoughts are often based on interpretations of things that happened in the past and on the decisions made then. A change in any of these three areas will automatically change the other two.

Elsie thought she had ruined her kids' lives because of her alcoholism. This thought was accompanied by feelings of guilt and hopelessness. She also believed that because of what she had done, she didn't deserve love from her kids. Her feelings of guilt, hopelessness, and the belief that she didn't deserve their love created avoidance actions. Elsie found it easier to hide out in depression than to spend time with her kids.

There are encouraging and discouraging patterns of thinking, feeling, and doing. Parents in recovery often allow guilt and shame to keep them in discouraging patterns of thinking, feeling, and doing.

A support group helped Elsie understand her discouraging patterns. Listening to others share how much they improved their relationships with their kids by focusing on what they could do now helped Elsie change her thinking. When she began to believe it was possible to change things in the present, she felt hopeful, and eager to spend loving time with her kids. As a result, at a family meeting she shared her sorrow and asked for forgiveness. She then asked the kids if they would be willing to help her plan special things to do together. Elsie was surprised at how willing her kids were to forgive her and how excited they were to plan special times.

If you are wondering if guilt and shame are running your life and leading you into self-defeating, discouraging patterns, the following checklist can help you look for clues. If you give yes answers to any of these questions, the signs of discouragement are present.

The Guilt and Shame Checklist
Clues to Discouraged Thinking:

1. Do I think about what I'm going to say before I say it, and do I censor saying things I believe others won't like hearing, or things that might get me in trouble?
2. Do I judge what others say instead of realizing they just have a different perspective from me?
3. Am I defensive when others tell me what they think?

4. Do I believe all the problems in the family are my fault?

5. Do I believe my mistakes are failures and that they can't be repaired?

Clues to Discouraged Feelings:

1. Do I confuse my feelings with my thoughts? When I talk about my feelings, do I say, "I feel like—" or "I feel that—" or "I feel you (or he, she, they)—"? (These phrases just lead us back to our thoughts. Feelings usually can be expressed with one word, as explained in Chapter 2.)

2. Do I try to cover up my feelings with food, spacing out, TV, or other new addictions?

3. Am I afraid to tell someone how I feel for fear it will give them power over me?

4. Do I display my temper by having tantrums or fits instead of just saying how I feel with dignity and respect?

5. Do I have a hard time knowing the name (one word) of my feelings?

Clues to Discouraged Behavior Patterns:

1. Do I refrain from asking for what I want and wait for others to read my mind to meet my needs?

2. Do I make excuses for others' disrespectful behavior instead of expecting them to be responsible and capable?

3. Do I pretend I don't feel the way I feel, or think the way I think?

4. Do I try to fix or control everything instead of working with others to find solutions we can all live with?

5. Do I refuse to forgive myself for past mistakes? Am I unwilling to say, "I'm sorry," or "I made a mistake?"
6. Do I allow others to abuse me physically or mentally?
7. Do I abuse others physically or mentally?
8. Do I spend too much time avoiding life while I space out in front of the TV, sleep too much, act depressed, and so on?

When you become aware of your discouragement, it can help you begin changes that can get you out of self-defeating patterns. You can begin to discover what works best for you—in your thinking, feeling, or behavior patterns. There is no one right method, but if you lack awareness that you are discouraged, you'll find it hard to know how to begin encouraging yourself and others.

Awareness Can Begin the Change Process

Most people in recovery have stories from their pasts that bring up feelings of guilt and shame. Dan was no exception. Dan never felt as if he "belonged" in high school unless he was hanging out with the partying crowd. When he got married, he and his wife did a lot of partying and drugging together. Dan used alcohol and drugs to numb his feelings.

When Josh, their first child, was born, Dan's wife became more responsible and decided to pull out of the partying crowd. On weekends, Dan wanted to get a sitter and go out and party, but she wouldn't hear of it. She wanted to stay home and be a family unit. When Dan's feelings of not belonging came up, he believed the only way he could feel accepted was to be in his partying group; so he went out without his wife.

Dan's drinking and drugging put a lot of strain on the family. When Dan was home, he was burned out. He avoided Josh because it felt like a burden to spend time and effort with his son. Dan and his wife argued a lot. There was verbal abuse on both sides and some physical abuse on his part.

When Josh was less than a year old, Dan and his wife separated. During the separation, when Dan took care of Josh he'd get stoned and smoke marijuana in front of him. As Josh got older he would ask what Dan was doing and Dan would say, "Smoking a cigarette." Once Dan was doing a line of coke, and Josh came in and said, "What are you doing, Daddy?" Dan said, "I don't know."

In addition to using a lot of drugs, Dan was also going from one relationship to the next. Josh would get close to a woman, and then either Dan or the woman would break up the relationship. It's hard for children to get attached and then have the relationship broken off—by someone else.

Dan knew he was neglecting his son because drugs came first with him. The quality of their time together was extremely poor. Many times, when it was his turn to care for Josh, he would stay up all night doing coke and alcohol the night before. When he picked Josh up the next day, he would be so tired and hung over that he would go to his folks' house and sleep all day while they took care of Josh.

As these patterns continued, Dan noticed Josh was pulling away from him. He often refused to let his dad hug him, and went to his room to play alone when Dan wanted to talk with him.

The Cost of Guilt and Shame

Whenever Dan thinks of the scene where his son watched him do drugs, or the times when he dumped his son on his parents, or the chaos he created by the many relationships his son had to deal with, he is filled with guilt and shame. Dan says that when he was using he wanted a high more than he wanted a marriage or his child. Being accepted by a group of friends and getting high simultaneously were more important to Dan than the needs of his child. He realizes that he abandoned and neglected Josh.

Now that Dan is sober and in recovery, he thinks he has to make up for all his past behavior by bending over backward to do what Josh wants. Dan thinks if he goes overboard to please his son that will make up for all the bad parts and drive away his feelings of guilt and shame.

Like many parents in recovery, Dan is certain that every problem he has with his now 5-year-old son is caused by what happened when he was using. Even when Josh acts like a normal, misbehaving 5-year-old, Dan is convinced it is his fault and that his son's behavior is caused by his past drug use.

Dan gives in to any demand Josh makes. When he has a nightmare and wants to sleep with Dan instead of in his bed, Dan is sure that Josh is feeling insecure because of past neglect. When Dan drives a hundred miles to spend the weekend with his son, and Josh changes his mind and wants to be with his friends instead of his dad, Dan is sure Josh is angry and punishing him for his old lifestyle. He turns around to head home without Josh, hating himself for his past failures.

Discouraged Thinking Patterns

If you look at Dan's unhealthy thinking patterns, you can see that they are discouraged because he believes he has caused his son's difficult behavior. He thinks it is his responsibility to make it up to Josh, so he doesn't expect Josh to behave. These thoughts are discouraging to both him and Josh because it keeps Dan feeling guilt, shame, and fear. Because of those feelings he acts in ways that spoil Josh—which is unhealthy for both of them. Dan's thoughts, feelings, and actions are all signs of self-defeating behavior.

Dan's behavior now is co-dependent. Instead of focusing on his drug of choice as he did when he was drinking and drugging, Dan is focusing on his son and trying to control Josh's life instead of living his own life. He treats Josh disrespectfully by acting as if there were a balance sheet in the relationship. Dan has decided that he is on the minus side of the balance because of past mistakes. Dan is forgetting about give and take in a healthy relationship. Instead of listening to his feelings and honoring his son's feelings, Dan thinks he has to fix everything and make it right. This kind of parenting invites Josh to be a manipulating brat whom Dan resents.

Parents in recovery sooner or later have to face the shame and guilt in order to get out of their discouragement. When they do that, they can start building healthier relationships.

Recognizing Self-Defeating Patterns to Begin Changing Beliefs, Feelings, or Actions Based on the Past

Dan began the change from unhealthy parenting to healthy parenting by recognizing the clues of his self-defeating patterns. This was the first step in learning how to care for himself and the beginning of the healing process. He used the knowledge of his self-defeating patterns to start building a healthy present and future.

Dan decided to change the weekend routine with his son. He called Josh to make plans for their weekend together. As usual, Josh said he didn't want to come to Dan's house. In the past Dan would have said, "OK," or "How about if I drive over? Maybe you'll change your mind." This time Dan said, "I think you are uncomfortable about coming to stay with me. It's OK to feel that way, but it's not OK not to come. Let's talk about what we can do to make it more comfortable for you."

Next, Dan changed the way he dealt with his feelings. In the past he held his feelings inside, but this time he spoke with emotional honesty. He allowed himself to experience what he felt, named the feeling, and told Josh exactly what was going on inside of him. Dan said, "I'm disappointed and hurt when you don't want to come over, because I enjoy spending time with you."

Josh said, "OK, Dad, I'll come." Dan was surprised that Josh responded so quickly and simply to his emotional honesty. Sharing your feelings honestly is powerful. Others often respond without manipulations or game playing.

Dan's third goal was to learn to be gentle with himself while making major changes in his thinking. He told himself, "I made a mistake and it's not the end of the world. I can admit my mistakes to myself and my child and move on. If I had known better, I would have done better. I have made a positive step by getting into recovery. I can continue learning to be a better parent one day at a time and in small steps. I can let my son know, by words or by actions, that I'm sorry. I am not a failure as a parent. I can learn new skills and move on, because mistakes are opportunities to learn."

In the beginning, it was uncomfortable for Dan to make changes, but he knew that more of his old thinking and behavior wouldn't make him feel better in the long run. He allowed himself the discomfort and continued to make changes based on faith that his new thoughts and actions would lead him and Josh to a more encouraging, healthy relationship.

Dan learned new parenting skills while he was in recovery so he could build a healthy relationship with his son. As Dan practiced these skills, his feelings shifted from guilt, shame, and fear to pride, comfort, and satisfaction. This allowed him to change his thinking about the past, forgive himself, and focus on today.

Dan now respects himself and models self-love and self-respect for his son. Dan told his son, "I feel ashamed of some of the things that happened when I was abusing drugs. Now that I'm clean and sober, I'm grateful for the opportunities I am creating to be the kind of father I really want to be. The past is past, but I can do something about the present."

Facing Fears, Sharing Shame, and Giving Up Guilt

Melanie gives us another example of facing fears, sharing shame, and giving up guilt. She described herself as a critical, bossy, mean parent who not only often embarrassed her kids with her drinking, but who also abdicated her responsibilities as a parent and let her 7-year-old daughter parent the family.

While Melanie was abusing alcohol, she felt constant pressure to cover up and hide her behavior so she wouldn't be exposed. Melanie could hear her kids laughing at her and treating her in a condescending way. She had so many accidents while driving in blackouts that her older children refused to get in the car with her. Melanie felt guilty about her behavior but didn't change it. Even though she lived in fear of getting caught, she didn't resist those extra drinks or the tirades at the kids when they made even the smallest mistake. On one occasion Melanie got so out of control that she exploded and slapped her 7-year-old across her face. Her older children looked on in horror and accused, "You tell us not to do that and *you're* doing it!"

One day Melanie took her daughter to the fair. She drank so much that she couldn't find her car and had to have her 7-year-old find it for her. Melanie finally became so embarrassed and ashamed that she went home and called a friend who gave her a number of someone in AA who would take her to a meeting that night.

Looking back at the checklist of clues of discouraged behavior, we can see that Melanie's thinking, feeling, and acting patterns were self-defeating. Melanie was guilty of neglecting her children when she was drinking.

Her kids and her extended family were sure that once she got into recovery, all that would change. When she stopped drinking and started attending AA meetings, they kept asking why she had to go to the meetings and told her she should be home with her kids. But just because Melanie started attending AA meetings didn't mean that her problems were over. Her biggest issue was taking time for herself and for personal growth.

By changing her thinking, Melanie was able to practice getting rid of guilt. She told herself it was OK to do what she wanted and needed, and to listen to her own thoughts and feelings instead of trying to please everyone else. She gave herself permission to heal herself first. She wanted to build her self-esteem so she had something to give to others.

By working on herself, Melanie was able to look at her ineffective ways of dealing with anger. She realized that when she felt guilty she soon felt resentful and angry and then took it out on the kids by berating or attacking them.

The Skill of Cooling Off

Melanie learned a skill called "cooling off" to get more in charge of her feelings. She stopped simply reacting to events, and took time to calm down and think about what was bothering her and how she might deal with it. Soon Melanie noticed that she wasn't taking personally everything her kids did.

The success Melanie experienced by changing her reactive behavior helped her change more of her thinking. She realized that she didn't have to be perfect and that progress was more important than perfection.

As Melanie kept practicing the use of a cooling-off period and took time to build up her self-esteem, her confidence grew. She realized she didn't have to make up for all that happened in the past. She accepted that the past was past and it was part of her. She wasn't perfect, and that was OK. Melanie broke her cycle of self-defeating behavior and learned to encourage both herself and her children.

Both Dan's and Melanie's stories are typical of people in recovery. By increasing their awareness of their self-defeating patterns of thinking, feeling, and doing, Dan and Melanie were able to build a more encouraging lifestyle for themselves and their children.

Using the Three R's of Recovery to Eliminate Guilt and Shame

The three R's of recovery (introduced in Chapter 1) give parents another tool, in addition to twelve-step work, to help develop self-forgiveness and to eliminate guilt and shame by dealing directly with people they have wronged.

Remember, the first R of recovery is to *recognize* you made a mistake. The second R is to *reconcile* by apologizing to the person who was wronged. The third R is to *resolve* the problem by working on a solution. In the following examples, Peggy uses the three R's of recovery to eliminate guilt and shame

When Peggy was a new mother, she was abusing alcohol. One day she needed a drink so badly that she started to shake uncontrollably. As she stood there shaking, her young baby fell off the changing table and Peggy heard the sound of the baby's head hitting the floor. Years later, whenever her daughter experienced any physical problems, Peggy could hear that sound. She was convinced every cold, asthma wheeze, and headache was her fault. No amount of alcohol could make that awful picture of her daughter's head hitting the floor go away. Even when Peggy got into treatment and recovery, her shame and guilt about this incident tore her apart.

When Peggy learned about the three R's of recovery from her therapist, she decided to go home to her daughter, now a teenager, and try them out. Peggy said, "Honey, when you were a baby, I made a horrible mistake that I still feel bad about. You know that I was abusing alcohol. I got the shakes so bad one day that I let you fall off the changing table and your little head hit the floor so hard! I can still hear the sound! I'm sorry I was so disrespectful to you and to myself, and I regret any pain this may have created for you. I wish it never had happened, because I've been in pain ever since, myself."

Peggy's daughter did what almost everyone does at this point. She gave her mother a big hug and said, "That's OK, Mom. I've always been a tough-headed kid, and I know you didn't mean for me to get hurt." Peggy asked if there was anything she could do to fix the damage and her daughter said, "Mom, I'm not damaged and it's really OK." In cases where actual damage has occurred parents can handle it the same way, focusing on what they can do in the present to deal with the feelings and/or consequences.

After that experience, Peggy still remembered the incident, but she had another picture that came quickly on top of the image. Now she could see her daughter hugging her and hear her saying, "It's OK, Mom." Peggy's guilt and shame slowly began to dissolve.

Healing the guilt and shame is a process. It is enhanced by becoming aware of discouraged thinking, feeling, and behaving patterns. The healing takes place when you accept that you are discouraged and know that you can change your thoughts and behaviors. You get healthier, and so does your family, when you are honest about your feelings and tell people how you feel, no matter how frightening that may be. You learn that it is scarier to think about what might happen than to actually open up and share the pain. Looking at old beliefs and decisions provides opportunities to change decisions, feelings, and actions that no longer serve you.

One day at a time, you can choose encouraging thoughts, feelings, and actions that are nurturing to the whole family. This doesn't mean you will be perfect and always be encouraging. A beautiful part of courage is making mistakes, recognizing them, and trying again. You can give this legacy of hope and courage to your children so they will have faith that they can handle whatever life presents.

Chapter
14

Make Sure the Message of Love Gets Through

Mrs. Russell became very upset when she found a six-pack of beer in her daughter's closet. She confronted Maria at the door with the six-pack of beer in her hand and demanded, "What *is* this?"

Bewildered, Maria answered, "It looks like a six-pack of beer to me, Mom."

Mrs. Russell said, "Don't get smart with me, young lady! I found this in your closet and you'd better explain."

Maria thought a minute before answering. "Oh yes, I remember. I was hiding that for a friend."

Mrs. Russell was incensed. "Do you expect me to believe that?" she screamed.

Maria shouted, "I don't *care* what you believe!" And she stormed off to her bedroom and slammed the door.

Later, Mrs. Russell shared this incident with a counselor

who was helping her with her recovery process. The counselor knew Mrs. Russell was overreacting with Maria because of her fear that Maria would follow her alcoholic path. The counselor also knew that one of the best ways to help her client get past her fears was to teach her the power of making sure the message of love gets through. She asked Mrs. Russell, "Why were you so concerned about the six-pack of beer?"

Mrs. Russell said, "Because I don't want her to get into trouble, like I did."

The counselor asked, "Why don't you want her to get into trouble like you did?"

Mrs. Russell thought this was a dumb question and answered with irritation, "Because I don't want her to ruin her life."

The counselor persisted: "And why don't you want her to ruin her life?"

Mrs. Russell couldn't believe the counselor could be so dense, and answered belligerently, "Because I love her!"

The counselor asked, "Do you think she got that message?"

As she got the point, Mrs. Russell looked chagrined and admitted, "Probably not."

What do you think? Did the message of love get through to Maria?

Perhaps a better question is, "Does it matter if the message of love gets through?" We believe it is extremely important that the message of love gets through to children. Only when they feel loved, can children hear parents and parents can have a positive influence. If the message of love doesn't get through, parents don't get through in any way that brings positive results. Parents deceive themselves when they think they are getting through to kids when they scold, lecture, humiliate, and punish.

Suppose Mrs. Russell had greeted Maria at the door and started with the message of love by saying, "Maria, I love you so much. When I found this six-pack of beer in your closet, I got real scared that maybe you are doing something that could hurt you or get you into trouble. Could we talk about this?"

Which approach would create the kind of closeness and trust that is inviting for communication and problem-solving? Obviously, the latter. The first approach creates distance and hostility, where communication and problem solving cannot take place. To invite closeness and trust, which create an environment that inspires growth and change, it is important to make sure the message of love gets through.

Seven Guidelines to Make Sure the Message of Love Gets Through

1. Create closeness and trust instead of distance and hostility. This creates an opening for positive influence.

2. Create a sense of understanding and validation by "getting into the child's world." This requires creative listening and sometimes guessing what he or she might be thinking or feeling.

3. Create a sense of fairness by taking responsibility, with dignity and respect, for whatever you have done to contribute to a problem. When you do, children will feel safe taking responsibility for their actions, with dignity and respect.

4. Create an atmosphere of mutual respect by having regular family meetings for compliments, shared feelings, and joint problem solving. When they feel needed and taken seriously, children feel loved and feel a sense of belonging and significance.

5. Create an atmosphere of encouragement by helping children understand that what they *do* is separate from *who* they are. When they know love is unconditional and they are treated with dignity and respect, children feel loved and develop courage.

6. Create confidence by welcoming mistakes as opportunities to learn and grow. When love does not depend on their performance, children feel loved.

7. Create courage and self-love by focusing on progress instead of on perfection. When they understand improvement is a lifelong process, children learn hope and faith in themselves.

Mrs. Russell could see that she had created distance and hostility by attacking Maria about the six-pack of beer. No wonder Maria had ended up in her bedroom with the door slammed shut. Mrs. Russell had experienced the short-term illusion of thinking she had been a responsible mother by confronting Maria about the beer. The long-term results were further damage to their relationship and no communication or solutions about the problem.

Mrs. Russell wanted to improve her damaged relationship with Maria. It made sense to her that she would not be able to get through to Maria until Maria felt loved. She wanted to establish closeness and trust so they could hear each other and know that love was the basis of their relationship. Mrs. Russell decided to try the "Seven Guidelines to Make Sure the Message of Love Gets Through."

When Maria came home from school the next day, Mrs. Russell greeted her at the door and asked in a loving tone, "Maria, could we talk?"

Maria still felt hurt and angry, so her tone was belligerent when she responded, "What do you want to talk about?"

Mrs. Russell maintained her attitude of love while she applied the skill of getting into Maria's world. She decided to make a guess about how Maria might be feeling. "When I started yelling at you about the six-pack of beer last night, I'll bet you thought I didn't even care about you."

Now Maria felt so understood and validated for her feelings that she started to cry. In a shaky voice, she confirmed her mother's guess: "It seems to me that I'm nothing but a bother to you lately and that only my friends really care about me."

Mrs. Russell further validated Maria's feelings by taking responsibility for her mistake: "I can see how it could seem that way to you when I come from my fear and start yelling at you instead of telling you the bottom-line truth about how much I love you and admitting that I'm just scared. Will you forgive me and give me another chance?"

Maria felt the love and her mother's sincerity, and melted. She put her arms around her mother and said, "It's OK, Mom. I've been pretty obnoxious too."

Mrs. Russell and Maria started having regular family meetings where they learned to solve problems together with dignity and respect for each other. During the compliment portion of the family meeting, they learned to notice and express the many things they appreciated about each other. The closeness and trust they created helped them feel the encouragement they needed to improve their self-love, love for each other, and to improve their behavior.

A Recovering Parent Learns to Make Sure the Message of Love Gets Through

Mae is another example of what can happen when a parent uses the "Seven Guidelines to Make Sure the Message of Love Gets Through." While she was using, Mae didn't respect herself. In recovery, Mae still didn't respect herself, because she didn't think she deserved respect. By following the "Seven Guidelines to Make Sure the Message of Love Gets Through," Mae learned to respect and love herself as well as her daughter Cheryl. This didn't happen overnight, but using the guidelines helped her have the courage to recover from the ups and downs of progress and regression.

Mae and her daughter Cheryl had been in a revenge cycle for years because of hurt, anger, guilt, and shame left over from Mae's years as an alcoholic. Mae is now a recovering alcoholic who has been sober since Cheryl was 12.

Mae's alcoholism became so severe when Cheryl was 5 that she gave up her role as a mother for over seven years and focused on her relationship with alcohol. After getting into recovery, her unresolved guilt for abandoning Cheryl and her two older brothers created more parenting mistakes. She tried to "make up" for her neglect in ways that invited Cheryl to decide she was entitled to take advantage of her mother.

Cheryl picked up cues from her mother and willingly played the guilt and shame game. She learned to have temper tantrums whenever she didn't get her way. Cheryl felt angry and revengeful about being abandoned, and had used that as an excuse to stay involved in drugs since she was 15. Even though Cheryl is now "grown up," she keeps manipulating her mother to give her "things" or to bail her out when she gets into trouble. Mae feels she can never be a good-enough mother and tries to make up for her failures by giving in to Cheryl's demands, hoping that will prove she cares.

Discouraged Belief Systems

Cheryl's behavior verifies that she has adopted many beliefs that might be typical for a youngest, only girl, who felt abandoned and who has two older brothers who are doing well in spite of (or maybe because of) the circumstances. She believes she can never do as well as her brothers; she believes that manipulation is the only way she can get what she wants; and she finds ways to blame others for whatever goes wrong in her life rather than taking any responsibility for the consequences of her choices.

Because Mae feels she is abandoning Cheryl again if she doesn't give her what she wants, she is inviting Cheryl to hold on to her "poor me" beliefs and continue her manipulating behavior. The results are extremely discouraging. Mae feels angry and resentful when she gives in to Cheryl's manipulations. She then strikes back by judging and lecturing Cheryl. Cheryl gives up and turns to drugs. Mae feels guilty and responsible for Cheryl's drug use. She feels hurt and resentful that her "giving tactics" and lectures don't work. In her discouragement, she gets even by avoiding Cheryl—so Cheryl feels abandoned. The cycle goes on and on.

Mae does not respect herself, nor does she show respect for Cheryl by giving in to her tantrums. While they are caught in this vicious cycle, the message of love does not get through.

Mae Asks for Help

Cheryl finally pushed Mae too far. She asked if she could clean the house "real good" for $40, at the end of a big holiday dinner. Mae agreed. When time came for the house to be cleaned, Cheryl decided she had time only for about 30 minutes of cleaning. Mae reminded her that the deal was for a thorough cleaning. Cheryl retorted angrily, "*You* wanted me to come to this family dinner! You *said* you would pay my way. I said I would clean the house just to help out, but I need to get out of here and get on my way!"

Mae gave in and let Cheryl have the $40, but she felt manipulated and resentful. That night Mae shared what had happened with her support group.

The support group helped Mae see that her two older sons now enjoy a good relationship with her in spite of the past. They helped her see that it is up to Mae and Cheryl to give up the past and get on with their lives. The group reminded Mae that she has the right to respect herself and that instead of looking for blame, it is time to look for solutions. They gave Mae an opportunity to participate in a role-play, where she played Cheryl while others helped her re-enact the housecleaning situation.

While role-playing Cheryl, Mae was surprised at how badly she felt about herself (as Cheryl) when she was able to con the person role-playing Mae. She certainly did not feel loved or lovable. Mae's insight was, "Good grief, I give in to her so she'll feel loved, but it has the opposite effect. I don't feel loving when I give in to her, and she doesn't feel loved. Wow!"

It was suggested that Mae replay the situation and be herself so she could practice new behavior based on her new insights. In the role play, when Cheryl started her tirade, Mae said, "Honey, do you know that I really love you?"

The person playing Cheryl acted startled, and then tried harder to continue the pattern of manipulation: "Then how come you always give my brothers more than you give me?"

Mae didn't take the bait. Instead she said, "Honey, I really love you, and I'll give you the $40 as soon as you clean the house thoroughly, as we agreed."

The person playing Cheryl stopped the role play and said, "I felt a little disgruntled about my old stuff not working, but deep down felt glad. I didn't really feel good about myself when I could get away with my con game. I felt really loved when Mae was loving, but firm."

Mae was able to see that when she gets past all her guilt and controls her own behavior, all she wants is to let Cheryl know that she loves her. It is up to Cheryl if she will receive that. She also discovered that when she starts with the foundation of making sure the message of love gets through, it is much easier to follow through on sticking to the agreement that both made.

Mae Gets Another Chance to Practice Self-Love and Mutual Respect

A year after the preceding incident Cheryl had reached bottom with her drug use. She moved in with Mae, her stepfather, and their three children, swearing that she was ready to turn over a new leaf. She was great for about a month, and then she started using and hanging out with her drug friends. Her behavior changed dramatically. She terrorized and manipulated the whole family with her temper tantrums, conning her stepbrothers and stepsister into loaning her money, leaving messes she would not clean up, staying out all night without letting anyone know where she was, and breaking all her promises to do her share around the house. Whenever Mae confronted her, she'd say, "It's your fault for being an alcoholic when I was a kid."

Mae regressed and slipped back into her co-dependent behavior and guilt feelings. She felt too discouraged to follow through and get Cheryl to keep her agreements. Mae said, "It was like a constant battle, a war. I kept trying to convince her to be respectful and keep her agreements. She kept trying to convince me it was all my fault. Nothing improved. I felt scared to leave the house because I didn't know what Cheryl would do to the house or to the other children. I felt like a prisoner in my own home!"

An Intervention

Cheryl's behavior became so unbearable that Mae finally went to a substance abuse treatment center to get help. The counselors there reminded her that she was enabling Cheryl by supporting her behavior. Mae was able to see that giving in to Cheryl's demands and guilt-provoking tirades was not helping her learn more productive skills. The treatment center also helped Mae see that Cheryl's behavior was largely influenced by her drug use and that she really needed help.

Shortly after Mae received this information, Cheryl did not come home for three days. Mae realized that she had an opportunity to respect herself by deciding what she would do instead of trying to change Cheryl. In the long run, Mae hoped her actions would create closeness and trust rather than distance and hostility. In order to do that, Mae would have to put up with some short-term tantrums and anger. She decided that what she had been doing wasn't working and that it was time to go back to what she knew about mutual respect.

Mae moved all Cheryl's stuff out on the porch with a long letter telling Cheryl she loved her but would no longer support her in the lifestyle she was choosing. She clarified that she would be happy to help her if she ever wanted to get into treatment.

Mae did not see Cheryl pick up her boxes of belongings, but they disappeared. A week later, Cheryl called Mae and wanted to have lunch. Mae went to meet Cheryl, determined she would not give in to her tantrums. She felt scared Cheryl would start yelling at her, blaming her, and putting her down. Mae almost fell over when Cheryl told her she would like to talk to the people at the treatment center.

Mae said, "I felt more closeness and trust than I had experienced in years. I think somehow Cheryl knew that I'd reached my bottom line and that loving her did not include allowing her to abuse me."

After talking with the staff at the treatment center, Cheryl decided to stay and complete their program. When Cheryl finished the 35-day treatment program, Mae felt she had her daughter back again. She reported, "I was so proud of her. I enjoyed her. I wanted to support and encourage her. I enjoyed being with her. She cooked, and cleaned house, and was so vivacious. She seemed real proud of herself, happy, hopeful, and optimistic."

"I can see now how unrealistic I was to believe that all of a sudden she'd become responsible. I wanted to believe all her stories that everything was different. I thought the way to help her was to have faith in her and believe her. So when she said she wanted to buy a car, I co-signed with her."

Within two months, Cheryl had relapsed into her drug use and her destructive behaviors. She stopped making her car payments. Mae learned a new lesson about mutual respect: Just because she showed respect for Cheryl didn't mean that Cheryl was ready to respect herself.

Mae relapsed into her guilt and enabling behaviors by paying for the car but recognized the mistake. She reminded herself that recovery is a process both for herself and her daughter. She remembered (again) it was best for her to control her own behavior by deciding what she would do instead of trying to make Cheryl different. She felt ripped off and angry about the car, and knew that she could let those feelings take her to revenge or to self-love. If she chose revenge, she would give in to Cheryl with resentment and keep making payments on her car. If Mae chose self-love and mutual respect, she would hold Cheryl accountable and respect herself enough not to let Cheryl take advantage of her.

Mae remembered that mistakes are opportunities to learn and grow. She realized she had made a mistake co-signing for the car. She found the car, took it to a dealer, and sold it to pay off most of the loan.

Cheryl tried every tantrum she could muster to get Mae to feel guilty and to buy her another car. Mae told Cheryl repeatedly, "I love you, and the answer is no." Mae had turned a corner. It wasn't easy, and it didn't happen overnight. By practicing self-respect, she was able to grow and let the message of love get through.

Mae is a good example of a parent who took two steps forward and one step backward several times—a familiar pattern for recovering parents. Eventually, lasting changes came about because Mae kept going back to the "Seven Guidelines for Making Sure the Message of Love Gets Through" to gain skills and strength in applying mutual respect. She found it helpful to make sure the message of love got through while remaining firm about giving up her co-dependent behavior. She said, "It is so much easier to say no when I say 'I love you' first."

This story does not have the kind of conclusion some people would like. We wish we could say that making sure the message of love got through was all it took for Cheryl to straighten out her life and live happily ever after. The truth is that Cheryl is still on drugs at this time. The improvement is that she no longer tries to manipulate Mae. Cheryl calls home once in a while, and the conversations are loving and respectful. Cheryl does not even ask for money or favors. Mae always expresses her love and says, "Call collect anytime. I love you, and I love to hear from you." Mae shared that she can love Cheryl unconditionally when she (Mae) doesn't worry about losing her self-respect by allowing herself to be manipulated. She now respects Cheryl's right to live her own life and learn her own lessons.

Mae also needed to live her own life and learn her own lessons. Parents need encouragement and self-love just as much as children. It will help if she focuses on progress instead of on perfection.

Parents in recovery often get discouraged if changes don't happen fast enough. They may forget that both parenting and recovery are processes that need to be approached one day at a time. Appreciating progress is more encouraging and realistic than expecting perfection. When parents see mistakes as opportunities to learn, they model self-love and courage for their children. Helping children know they are not bad when they make mistakes and instilling them with the hope that they can learn from mistakes is one of the most beautiful messages of love. It is a message worth giving to yourself as well as your children.

All the "Seven Guidelines for Making Sure the Message of Love Gets Through" can be valuable to recovering adults as well as to children. They can help you develop the self-love and self-respect that might have been missing from your childhood. The beginning of self-love and self-respect is welcoming mistakes as opportunities to learn and grow. The past is the past. Now is now. Remember that self-love does not depend on your performance. Poor performance does not give you an excuse to stay the same. It does offer you hope to continue learning and growing.

You create courage, self-love, and self-respect by focusing on progress instead of perfection. Like your children, you need the hope and faith in yourself that comes from understanding that improvement is a lifelong process.

It feels good to take responsibility for your actions with dignity and respect. When you leave blame and shame out of responsibility, you are left with a sense of freedom and creativity. You see that you created your behavior and you can change it. You feel good about yourself when you learn problem-solving skills in family meetings to help you make changes.

In several chapters, we have discussed the importance of understanding beliefs and feelings as a key to understanding behavior. You need to check into your own worlds as well as the worlds of your children. You can listen creatively to your feelings and explore the information contained in your early memories.

As long as you practice self-respect, you can protect yourself from becoming a victim or a bully. In most cases no one can mistreat you if you don't allow it, and you can respect others' rights to dignity and respect, even if you are unhappy with their behavior.

If you lose your self-respect and allow an addict to make your life unbearable and hurt your children, you may need to consider the option of getting away from the abusing spouse. Separation and/or divorce may be necessary. Staying in a bad relationship for the sake of the children backfires when you allow your children to be constantly verbally abused or physically or sexually abused. If you are in an abusive relationship, get outside help to make the important changes and decisions that are needed to bring health to the family. This is a way to show self-love.

You can create closeness and trust within, as well as with your children. The self-love and self-respect that comes from feeling closeness and trust within fills your cup so you have more to give.

Making sure the message of love gets through is the greatest gift you can give your children. They form their opinions of themselves through their perception of how you feel about them. When they feel loved and feel a sense of belonging and significance, they have the foundation on which to develop their full potential to be happy, contributing members of society. Your positive influence gets through when your message of love gets through.

Index

257

forms of, 63–64
growth process, 56–57
interdependence goal, 56–58
patterns, 55–64
resistance to change, 62–63
support groups, 40–41
Co-Dependents Anonymous
  (CODA), 72
Comic relief, 156
Communication,
  clarify thoughts, 107–108
  closed system, 102
  conflict resolution skills,
    108–110
  defined, 97
  effective about drugs, 117–119
  honest, 118
  horizontal, 98–99
  informative, 118
  joint problem solving,
    110–116
  listening, 103–105
  love guidelines, 243–245
  love message, 241–255
  nonjudgmental, 119, 129–135
  nonverbal, 26–27, 110, 122
  one-up-manship, 98
  open, 119
  practicing respectful, 99–100
  quiz, 99
  recovering family, 99–102
  skills, 97–116
  "the three yeses," 105–107
  unhealthy, 97–98, 103
  verbal message, 122
  vertical, 98–99
Competition, sibling, 149
Compliments, family, 15
Conflict resolution, 108–116
Connecting with outside
  support groups, 31–54
"Cooling off," 238
Co-parenting skills, 207,
  216–217

Decide for yourself, 207, 215–216

Defensive attitude, 25–26
Deflating to inflate
  communication, 98
Dependence, to interdependence,
  56–57, 60–62
Dependency, chemical, 1
Dependent person, defined, 8
Despair, 181
Diagnostic clues, mistaken
  goals, 171–172
Dignity, 11–12. See also Respect
Dinner time routines, 75–78
Discouraged,
  behavior patterns, 230–231
  belief systems, 247
  feelings, 230
  guilt and shame checklist,
    229–231
  thinking, 229–230, 234
Discouragement, 169
Discovery, defined, 189
Doing for, 94–95
Doing to, 94–95
Doing with, 94–95
Dreikurs, Rudolph, 98, 169–170,
  223
Drugs,
  blackout, 140, 237
  cocaine, 7, 27, 40–41, 121–122,
    193, 231–232
  decision to use, 120–124
  early adolescents, 133–135
  education, 124–125
  effective communication,
    118–120
  experimental use, 129–133
  marijuana, 122, 130–131, 193
  nonjudgmental information,
    129–135
  polydrug abuse, 193, 195,
    231–232
  preschool children, 124–126
  primary grades, 126–133
  signs of use, 135–136
  teens, 136–145. *See also*
    Chemical abuse

BOOKS AND TAPES AVAILABLE
FROM JANE NELSEN, LYNN LOTT, AND RIKI INTNER

To: Sunrise Books, Tapes & Videos   Telephone: 1/800/456-7770
    P. O. Box B / Provo, UT 84603   (orders only, please)

Please send the following:

BOOKS	Price	Quantity	Amount
CLEAN & SOBER PARENTING: A Guide to Help Recovering Parents by Jane Nelsen, Riki Intner, and Lynn Lott	$10.95	_____	_____
I'M ON YOUR SIDE: Resolving Conflict With Your Teenage Son or Daughter by Jane Nelsen and Lynn Lott	$ 9.95	_____	_____
RAISING SELF-RELIANT CHILDREN IN A SELF-INDULGENT WORLD by H. Stephen Glenn and Jane Nelsen	$ 9.95	_____	_____
POSITIVE DISCIPLINE: Teaching Children Self-Discipline, Responsibility, Cooperation, and Problem-Solving Skills (Nelsen)	$ 9.95	_____	_____
UNDERSTANDING: Eliminating Stress and Finding Serenity in Life and Relationships (Nelsen)	$ 9.95	_____	_____
TIME OUT: Abuses and Effective Uses (Nelsen and Glenn)	$ 6.95	_____	_____
POSITIVE DISCIPLINE STUDY GUIDE (included with *Positive Discipline Video*)	$ 6.00	_____	_____
MARRIED AND LIKING IT (Lott and West)	$ 7.95	_____	_____
FAMILY WORK: Whose Job Is It? (Lott, Intner & Kientz)	$ 9.95	_____	_____
TO KNOW ME IS TO LOVE ME (Lott)	$10.00	_____	_____
TEACHING PARENTING (Lott with Allen)	$40.00	_____	_____

VIDEOS

POSITIVE DISCIPLINE VIDEOS (Two One-Hour Videos and Study Guide)	$49.95	_____	_____

CASSETTE TAPES

POSITIVE DISCIPLINE (Nelsen)	$10.00	_____	_____

SUBTOTAL _____

UT and CA residents add 6.25% sales tax _____

Shipping and handling: $2.50 first item; $.50 each item thereafter _____

TOTAL _____

(Prices subject to change without notice.)

METHOD OF PAYMENT (Check One):

_____ Check or Money Order Made Payable to **SUNRISE, INC.**

_____ Mastercard   _____ Visa

Card # ____ ____ ____ ____   Expiration Date _____/_____

Ship to _____

Address _____

City/State/Zip _____

Daytime Phone _____